It's Time...
for Change

How making positive changes will enhance your spiritual life

Aruna Ladva

IT'S TIME ... FOR CHANGE
How making positive changes will enhance your spiritual life
Aruna Ladva

Copyright © 2014 BKIS Publications, London

PRINT ISBN: 978-1-886872-45-5
KINDLE ISBN: 978-1-886872-46-2
EPUB ISBN: 978-1-886872-47-9

First published in 2014 by Brahma Kumaris Information Services Ltd,
Global Co-operation House, 65 Pound Lane, London, NW10 2HH
Website: www.bkpublications.com
E-mail: enquiries@bkpublications.com

The right of Aruna Ladva to be identified as the Author of the Work
has been asserted by her in accordance with the Copyright, Designs
and Patents Act 1988.

1 3 5 7 9 10 8 6 4 2

All rights reserved. No part of this book may be reproduced by any
mechanical, photographic or electronic process, or in the form of
a photographic or audio recording, or stored in a retrieval system,
transmitted or otherwise copied for public or private use without the
written permission of the publisher. Requests for permission should
be addressed to: BK Publications, Global Co-operation House,
65 Pound Lane, London, NW10 2HH

Illustrations by Joachim Debarge
Designed by Makar Publishing Production, Edinburgh
Printed by CPI Group (UK) Ltd., Croydon, CR0 4YY

Contents

Introduction	ix
Values are Caught Not Taught	1
Waste Not, Want Not	4
Renaissance	8
Mood Management	10
Every Second Counts	14
Colour Your Life	17
Healing the Heart	19
Staying Clear of Gossip	22
Don't Take Sorrow and Don't Give Sorrow	24
Thoughts Become Things	27
Minding Our Language	31
Less is More	34
Making an Appointment with Yourself	36
Sulk Not – Smile a Lot	39
Back to Basics	42
Think Less, Do More	46
Spiritual Warrior	49
Student Life is the Best	52
Imagery	56
Full Stop	59
Dying to be Thin	62
Spiritual Bypass	66

Take Off Your Shoes	69
The 'W' Perspective	71
Travelling Light	74
Understanding Death	77
Lifting the Veil of Illusion	80
The Birth of Desire	83
Honesty is the Best Policy	87
In God's Heart	90
About the author	93
About the Brahma Kumaris	94
How and where to find out more	95

The message is loud and clear, take the initiative for positive change or else the world will surely change you.

Introduction

If time changes me then time is my master, but if I change before time, then I am the master.

To be able to choose and initiate change in one's life is a very empowering feeling because it confirms that I am in control of my tomorrow. This is mastery over the self – and the real meaning and purpose of Raja Yoga. It is also the reason why I love pursuing this magical journey of self-improvement.

As we change, we find that people around us begin to respond to us differently. I have experienced this numerous times. Whenever I decide to move on, or to let go, or to adjust, I notice a shift around me.

I feel greatly blessed to be living this life, at the same time I know that, had I not done the 'inner work', things would not be as they are. Genuine transformative change has to be initiated from inside.

All of us are, to a greater or lesser degree, stuck in old patterns of thinking and behavior, and this blinds us to myriad opportunities of learning and growing. Or we may even be aware of our shortcomings and have the desire to change, but perhaps we just don't quite have the formula.

To have a rigid attitude is a painful way of being. Living in confusion, fear or low self-esteem is not comfortable either. However there are solutions to these challenges if we seek to find them. When we have the will, and we apply some understanding and effort, then we can really begin to shape and direct our life.

The human race is passing through a critical period in its journey, as evidenced by increasing conflict on a domestic to a global scale. We can either be adversely affected by this climate of anxiety and fear, or we can be agents for change. With every choice we make, there is an outcome that changes the world for better or worse.

I believe that at this special time we are being called to emerge our higher potential. We are being asked to use our initiative and take the lead in re-creating harmony and balance in the world. Not in an arrogant way, but in a responsible way. It only takes a few to create light amidst the darkness just as one small candle in a darkened room is enough to show the way out.

It's Time...for Change is for those seekers of truth who do not want to simply live in denial or sweep issues under the carpet. It is for those who have a compelling desire to look inside more deeply and consciously choose to change.

Embrace Change!

Values are Caught Not Taught

Values are at the bottom of everything we do. They determine a lot of what we attempt and accomplish in our lives. If we give weight and importance to something we will give it time and energy. But can values really be taught, or are they passed on from one generation to another through inspiration and perspiration!

If you were asked to place a monetary value on yourself, what would you reply? How much are you worth? If your child needed some time with you, what would you quote him or her – how much is your time worth? How much would one need to pay to get some honesty out of you. Or perhaps there is a special deal on respect this week but NOT love! It's not to do with the monetary value. It relates to the denomination of one's self worth!

In fact, values lie in the heart of every soul regardless of whether we can 'feel' them or not. Each time we make a decision a value is at play. Sometimes love, care and concern, generosity, peace, or we may exercise negative values but then that would be an oxymoron. What concerns us here are the values that give value and worth to the soul.

Values earn us blessings. The tidings of love help to oil the wheels of our lives and make them smoother. Success and victory arrive easily. Values earn us loyalty and friendship. Values earn us more money as we demonstrate trust and honesty. Values earn us fidelity and dignity. This income is endless and at the same time priceless.

It's Time... to Change

Our conscience relies totally on our set of values. If our core values are justice and fairness, then we will ensure that is reflected in our every action. If our key value is sweetness, we will ensure that we do not hurt others. Otherwise, our conscience will surely be troubled. In other words, it will speak out and tell us that what we are about to do is not in alignment with our 'real' self, our higher self. Listening to our conscience is a big part of exercising and asserting our values.

How much something is worth depends on how much you value it! You may not value somebody until you really need them. And in that situation, you may be willing to pay exorbitant sums of money for the object of your desire. Thus the value of something is also rated on the need of the moment.

When we respect our own selves, we are functioning from our core values of love, truth, kindness, respect, peace and joy. This is what gives value or importance to the soul. A person filled with values is likely to earn more on all levels, as employers are not just looking for the academic credentials, but also soul qualities.

With so much deceit and corruption floating around there is no better time to act out of value and virtue. Many people say they have to lie to make money or conduct their business, but money earned in that way is deceiving you into thinking you own it – very soon it will leave your hands as fast as it came.

IT'S TIME... to share our values: unity, simplicity, cooperation, tolerance, humility, love, peace, respect, freedom and more – they cannot be enforced, only exemplified. Value your life and all personal resources – we know that money can't buy life, but the blessings and good wishes of others have certainly proven to heal the soul and body. We know that a palace is not everything, if it does not have the atmosphere of love and peace. We also know that a five-course meal is not satisfying if not eaten with friends and family. Try giving a thirsty person in the dessert a treasure chest full of gold, and he will be willing to trade it in for a glass of water; the treasure chest will have no value!

Waste Not, Want Not

'Waste not, want not' is a well-known English expression; yet how conscious are we of the amount of waste we generate throughout the day, every day? Waste is not only that which shows up in our rubbish bins at the end of the day. There are other, more subtle forms of waste that deplete us of our soul energy, and then we wonder where we went wrong!

Firstly, 'waste' is a relative term. What might be waste to one person may be a necessity to another. So we should not stand and judge whether someone is wasting something or not. First rule of thumb – look at yourself first!

Secondly, as we waste our resources that are entrusted to, or bestowed upon us, we are creating subtle negative karmic accounts. Our time is a resource, our wealth, the people around us, Mother Nature... So, if I waste my time, for example, then that moment is lost forever, and perhaps too, an opportunity that may not come again. If I waste my money, then money won't come to me when I really need it.

The law of karma states that what I give out, I get back – both positive and negative. The same law applies here: if I do not use time, thoughts, or things in a worthwhile way, then they won't be there for me when I need them. Let's explore some of the ways in which we waste our personal assets and resources and then how we can maximize them to create better karma!

Thoughts

How many thoughts do we create throughout the day? *Time* magazine stated once that it is something like 60,000. Yet how many of them are useful and necessary? If I am creating thoughts that are 'extra', or on top of a decision already taken, then they would fall into the category of waste.

If there are repetitive thoughts, or thoughts of worry or doubt, these are not helpful and drain the mind of its energy. In that moment, I am misusing my mind, which creates heaviness, sadness, moodiness or headaches. I now have a mind that is uncooperative, very much like an upset child, who is obstinate and unwilling to behave the way I want it to. Through meditation we learn to become the masters of our minds, and this is why a yogi is blessed with happiness – they do not allow themselves to be taken hostage by an excess of negative or waste thoughts.

Words

With the advent of mobile phones, facebook, Twitter and Skype – the so called social media – we have more opportunities than ever to 'chat'. Despite our over-busy lives, chatting is something that most of us still find plenty of time to do. Yet how many of our words are really meaningful, useful and worthwhile? Do we use a dozen words when two will do, or repeat the same stories ten times over? Worse still, is some of our time spent talking about others in a less-than-complimentary way? Beware! Your words will come back to you!

Even silence can speak volumes! Taking time to consider and choose your words means that the words you do speak are much more likely to be listened to!

If that is not enough to convince you, remember that approximately less than 10% of face to face communication is through words, our body language actually speaks much louder!

Money

Money is something that most people complain they don't have enough of, however if the same people were asked to keep an account of their outgoings for a month, they may well see that a lot of expenditure is unnecessary. Do we always need to have the latest phone or designer watch, rendering the previous ones useless in an instant? Of course we are free to use our hard-earned cash as we wish, but be careful not to fill a huge karmic wastebasket along the way!

Unbridled spending, you may have noticed, brings sorrow, not happiness. However, hoarding money selfishly is not healthy either. Learn to discern the 'needs' from the 'wants', use your money for good reasons and good causes, be generous to others, spend it wisely, and you will find it comes back to you.

Relationships

Sometimes we take relationships for granted; not valuing the other persons time, their intelligence, kindness or presence. Everyone has a gift to offer to the world, if I can't see it, then that is my mistake.

Relationships are an investment – what you put in, you get out. If you are taken advantage of, perhaps you have taken advantage of another? If you are blessed and cared for, it must be that you have sent that energy out before which is why it is rippling back. So often, when a loved one dies, the bereaved is wracked with guilt or sorrow because they didn't express their feelings when that person was still alive. The lesson is clear – don't wait to tell someone how much you appreciate them!

Natural Resources

We know the earth has been plundered almost to a point of no return. We can do our best to reduce, recycle and reuse, but is that enough?

Actually, if we respect Mother Nature, she will respect us. The more we help in sustaining the planet, the more the planet will find ways to help us. It will take a huge collective effort to save the world, but individually our contribution does make a difference on many levels. If I squander resources, karma says that they won't be there for me at a time of need. If I look after them as a trustee, a guardian, then I am creating a relationship of harmony with the elements.

IT'S TIME... to use your treasures of time, energy, relationships and resources in a worthwhile way. The two keywords are appreciation and respect. Appreciate what you have and make the most of it; respect what has been given to you and it will serve you well! Then you'll notice how rarely you have to empty your 'karmic trash bin'.

Renaissance

After centuries of false notions, the ideal of human power and potentiality was reborn in a period known as the Renaissance. The dramatic transformation of worldview from the medieval era went hand in hand with a number of discoveries, innovations and improvements. The world was no longer flat, as deemed before, and men and women were encouraged to broaden their thinking and create a much more open outlook. As we reflect on world history, we realize that periods of Renaissance in fact resulted in freedom of speech and action, as we broke through old molds of thinking and behavioral patterns.

Renaissance comes from the combination of the French verb *renâitre*, meaning 'to revive or rebirth' and Italian *Rinascimento*, from *ri-* 'again' and *nascere* 'be born'. And so after generations of knowledge and information, many of us are answering an inner call: to rediscover, reinstate, re-establish, revive, restore, renew, repair, renovate and reinvent our lives. Old paradigms are crumbling and new ones are rapidly constructed in their place. However, despite the world's largest library at our fingertips, we have yet to find our own truth, and further, have time to live it. The message is loud and clear, change or else the world will surely change you.

Leonardo da Vinci, the pioneer of Renaissance, taught us 'curiosita' – an insatiably inquisitive approach to life and an unrelenting quest for discovery and learning. He taught us to question profusely and to also change the form of questioning from time to time. For example, instead of asking how we can get to water (the water well), he said ask, 'how can we get water to come to us'. This was the start of the underwater pipeline!

The spiritual Renaissance that is dawning today asks us all to begin an inner journey, one where we take time to absorb all that history tells us about ourselves, and to re-discover and revere the leader within by taking full control and responsibility for our life. We need the courage to question old attitudes and archetypal ways of thinking that aren't working for us. To find new ways of living this fast-track life and even more importantly, to enjoy it!

IT'S TIME... to embrace the same 'curiosita' for the self; this voracious pursuit of self-discovery. Ask your self: 'Am I a human doing, or a human being?' 'Is peace realized through sound or silence?' 'How is greater happiness attained, through giving or receiving?' Re-awaken the enormous potential that is lying dormant within, and you will witness the birth of a new you!

Mood Management

Moods play a major role in our lives. They govern our feelings and actions and, if not managed well, can create havoc and chaos in our minds leading to depression and other mental illnesses. Do you find that something as simple as the weather or the morning headlines can alter your mood?

Moods are basic psychological states that can occur as a reaction to an event or can surface for no apparent external cause. A mood is an internal, subjective state. It is also a relatively long lasting emotional state. Moods differ from emotions in that they are less specific, less intense and less likely to be triggered by a particular stimulus. People speak of being in a good mood or a bad mood and this often lasts for days and not hours as in the case of a feeling or an emotion. Moods also differ from temperament or personality traits which are long lasting.

Moods can manipulate how individuals interpret and translate the world around them, and can also direct their behavior. In a study done by Niedenthal and Setterlund (1994), research showed that individuals are tuned to perceive things that are congruent with their current mood. Both the pessimist and optimist will prove themselves right as they manifest what they have interpreted through the lens of their mood!

According to psychologist Robert Thayer, mood is a product of two dimensions: energy and tension. A person can be energetic or tired while also being tense or calm. According to Thayer, people feel best when they are in a calm-energy mood, and worst when in a tense-tired state. The low energy arousal coupled with tension, as experienced in a bad mood, can be counteracted by walking. Thayer suggests walking as a means to enhanced happiness (*Wikipedia*, 2011).

Research has shown that, contrary to the stereotype of the suffering artist, creativity is enhanced most by positive moods and happy thoughts.

People have often used food to regulate mood. Take for example chocolates – yes, that dark gold bar of pure happiness! The benefits of dark chocolate come from resveratrol, an antioxidant and immune system booster. It also has the ability to boost brain levels of endorphins as well as serotonin, a mood-altering chemical on which many antidepressants act. The recommended dose however is only one ounce per day, so remember not to over indulge.

German researchers studying garlic's effect on cholesterol discovered that participants being treated with garlic experience an elevation in mood. Now this does not necessarily mean good mood, as it also implies that one can become e-motional – 'energy is in motion' – and perhaps not one in control! Pilots are advised not to eat garlic up to 72 hours before flying as it slows down concentration and doubles or triples reaction time. Knowing what to eat is an important part of *food-mood management!*

Music can also alter moods. Niedenthal and Setterland used music to induce positive and negative moods. Sad music was used as a stimulus to induce negative moods, and participants labelled other things as also negative. This proves that people's current moods tend to affect their judgment and perception in all areas of their lives. Surround yourself with music that will uplift your spirits and not strip the light of your aura.

People who tend to be moody are less predictable and difficult to work with. They are needy, stroppy, self–centered, procrastinators and susceptible to sulking. People are less inclined to want to work with them as the other party is not always sure of how they may react and so they hesitate to even ask them for favours. People who have a stable and consistent mood make the best leaders. They have a focus and consistently keep their vision well oiled.

The difference between a response and a reaction is that a 're-s-ponse' is thought out or pondered over whereas a re-action is to re-enact something that has taken place previously. For example… you begin your day with an argument with your spouse. On your way to work you mull over this incident in your mind. By the time you get to work, the receptionist greets you with a big bright smile and at that moment you ask her in an irritated tone, what has she got to smile about! The anger built up from an earlier incident is brought forward to the present incident; you have brought forward the anger. Part of learning to manage moods is to be able to segregate incidents in our mind and not to let them overlap.

Sickness and ill health can also make a person short-fused and less tolerant. We become vulnerable and susceptible – knee jerk reactions. When the body is sick, we have to ensure the mind is not! And so for times like this, we need to be sure that we have acquired enough power through meditation that will assist us at a time of need. The healing process will be faster if we maintain the right attitude!

Hormones also play a major part in understanding why certain moods erupt at certain times. Coupled with modern day stress, it creates anarchy in the soul. Learning to understand the workings of the mind and body is the key to prevention.

The atmosphere of a place can also induce certain moods. Walk into a church or hospital, funeral parlor or shopping mall and you certainly won't be feeling the same way inside. Know what you want and surround yourself with healthy and positive people and be selective about the places you frequent.

Mood Management

IT'S TIME... to take responsibility and not allow external factors to affect your mood. As a master of your mind and body, take time to understand what triggers your moods. Play some light music every day to soothe your soul. Eat your meals in a mindful state. And slow down before you end up in a mood ditch that is hard to get out of!

Every Second Counts

There is a great deal to learn from sports. If we would invest just as much time learning from it as we do watching it, we would indeed be enriched! All forms of sportsmanship require a deep spirituality; focus and concentration are the keys to winning and striking the target!

In cricket every run is important, in running every sprint, in tennis every point, in swimming every lap, in basketball every net, etc. Being behind a few points, may not matter at first, but this small lead is enough to give your opponent the confidence to gallop ahead and then you are forever playing catch up or as in chess forever trying to free up your pieces for the rest of the game.

Where the game is time sensitive, every second is crucial and cannot afford to be wasted. Records are broken by the second. The difference of winning or losing can be determined in a fraction of second. And the winner cannot allow their vision to be distracted or to go astray for even a second. For the winner, the destination, the target, the aim is right there in front of their eyes.

In daily life too, every second is an opportunity to win hearts. It's totally in our hands how we hold the 'bat' and in which direction we hit the 'ball'! Love and friendship needs to be won with love and blessings and not coercion and compulsion. Sometimes, we feel it's not in our hands, but is that really true. Do people not respond to us in the way we treat them?

Every thought creates every moment, every hour, every day and every week. As we think, so we create our present reality.

Every Second Counts

We may believe it's just one negative thought, but before we know it, it has taken hold of our feelings and emotions and there is a resistance in our actions.

Real life is a bit different from sport, where the only objective is to outdo your opponent and win at any cost. If we create the same rules of win/lose in our personal lives then our premise will be that one has to lose in order for the other to win. In daily life, however, since we are vying for the heart which is more encompassing and embracing, win/win outcomes are indeed possible and we just have to learn to 'serve' generously and graciously with our feelings!

Relationships are indeed an investment and will reap generous dividends if I have invested prudently. Constantly withdrawing from the balance will not leave me much 'at a time of need'. I need to ensure that I am giving and not just taking, or if I have taken, then to ensure to return something back immediately before the account depletes too quickly. But the winner takes a step further; he does more than the average, he gives more of himself than the average athlete!

If people seem to be playing games with you, then choose not to be against them, choose not to be their opponent – this is exactly what gives them power over you; one-upmanship. Most conflict occurs when there is an opposition created, a rivalry, a 'them' and an 'us', you versus me. But if we can see ourselves on the same side, two people wanting the same thing – then we are not enemies, but partners. We both want the same thing; we are just going about it from different angles. So take courage and change the rules of the game!

Timing is also pivotal in 'triumphing' in relationships; it takes a certain spiritual discernment to know what to say, as well as when and how to say it. What will be that prize-winning word or statement that will touch the soul, secure trust and launch an alliance? Sometimes due to our embarrassment or ego we miss the opportunity to say what we genuinely wanted to say and that moment is lost forever.

There is a saying in Islam that we have a limited number of breaths. So we better start using them wisely, for every breath gone shall never return. In several other faiths they also speak of taking God's name in every breath, thus every breath will matter when I am eventually in front of God and the account has to be settled.

Sometimes accepting defeat is also part of the game. We may have lost the battle, but we have not lost the war. We may have lost the argument, or lost the match, but we can learn from the surfer who knows there will always be another wave!

IT'S TIME... to pay attention to every thought, every second, to every moment and every breath, for the winner pushes himself more than the average athlete. In every breath let me remind myself that I am a soul, a point of light, a radiant energy, and glowing, shining and a mirror to spread God's light. Give more than you take. And don't become hopeless because another wave is on its way right now!

Colour Your Life

The colours of the rainbow speak volumes and nature has its own language for communicating with us and lighting up our life through colour. Imagine for a moment what our world would be like if we only had black and white, and the in-between shades of gray. Each colour has its own vibrational frequency. Yellow represents sunshine, happiness and creativity; red – strength and courage; blue – patience and stability; pink – love and compassion; purple – royalty and power; green – healing, growth and prosperity; and white is a symbol of truth, purity and cleanliness.

Any decorator or designer will tell you how important colour is in our lives. People's interest in colour therapy has increased enormously in recent years. It is true that by looking at certain colours, or being surrounded by them, either through wall coverings or flowers and fabrics, there is an influence on the moods of the soul.

Since the face is the mirror of the mind, moods do without doubt reflect through the 'colour', i.e. the state, of our being. For example, when sick, we are pale. When pleased, we are as 'pink as peach' and when shy we go 'red as a tomato'. But is it really possible to change moods simply by sitting in front of a colour?

The colour of the soul has to be changed from within, inside out. Weak and negative thoughts such as doubts, fears and worries 'cloud' our soul and 'dull' our moods, a bit like adding a drop of colour into a pot of pristine white paint. It loses its radiance, its purity. When caught up in the shadow of our own negativity, the world can seem colourless, without beauty or

 **It's Time...** *to Change*

radiance. It is in those moments that we need to remember that every cloud has its silver lining and the 'Sun' light is not far away, it was just hidden from view for a while.

Each virtue is like a colour we apply to ourselves; the more we use virtues and positive qualities in our lives, the more we deepen the tint on the soul. By emerging more and more virtues, we light up our lives, and radiate that light unto others. Every one of us has our own special vibration, our unique combination of colours, textures and patterns. Our life is in our hands and we can weave a masterpiece.

IT'S TIME... to get out the paintbrush of your life and enliven your world! Paint boldness and courage. Paint love, kindness and compassion. Paint joy, celebration and thankfulness for the unlimited colour palette that the world offers to us to choose from. And guess what? When we are complete with the full spectrum of virtues – a compound of all the colours of the rainbow – we arrive back at white – simplicity and peace!

Healing the Heart

We live in a broken world, many of us nursing broken hearts, living half a life as our soul remains asleep. A broken heart is not about romantic love, though that opens a fissure within that can lead to deeper realizations. The brokenness here is about us not being whole people: body and soul.

For many of us the heart is more than just a physical organ, it combines the physical and metaphysical and symbolizes a universal emotion that transcends all languages – LOVE. If our heart were to stop, then our life would end, as would our zest and joy for life, and joy and love are the gateway to experiencing the depths of the soul.

For so long we silenced our heart, and let our mind and intellect control us. During the reign of our mind, we have waged war against each other, fought within our families and loathed ourselves as we try to compete and compare. All violence starts in the minds (not in the hearts!) of man. At its worst, mankind has lived purely in the physical realm, seeing only tangible goals and victories, blinded to the suffering around or within; shutting out emotions. We experience fear and justify our wars and battles based on prejudices, ignorance, and a need to control – all functions of the mind. When we operate solely from the mind then we lose our peace, because peace dwells only in the heart. Where only peace resides, then fear cannot be present.

The heart takes us from the temporal into the unlimited, from the measurable to the infinite, and from logic to emotions. The heart reminds us that we are spiritual beings experiencing life through our bodies, the physical. When we silence the heart

and only listen to the mind we essentially cut ourselves off from the life-affirming energy of our inner truth.

In most so-called developed countries today heart disease is a leading cause of death. Some believe that a 'heart attack' is synonymous with a 'spiritual crisis'. As we look at the signs of a world under siege, 'spiritual heart attacks' are becoming an epidemic. Our greatest strengths are experienced when we balance the energies of the mind (logical) and our heart (emotional and spiritual). When we live once again by our core values of love, peace and truth, then we will always be guided back to safety. The mind has its role, but for it to function well it must be connected to the heart, that inner voice, our intuition. In each of us is the cure for our present ills; and that is to listen to our heart and start our journey to wholeness. Healing is a process, a journey of self-discovery and one of love. Doctors and science may be able to remove the pain of the body but not the sorrow of the soul. For this we have to become our own healers.

Many give their healing a deadline or rush to a quick fix cure. It's known that patients, who begin to acknowledge their part in the healing process are the ones who recover fastest. They are no longer focused on themselves nor feeding their dis-ease with old habits or useless thought patterns from the past. In addition to awakening their soul and feeling the warmth of that love, they also tend to discover a purpose. The joy of helping and sharing is therapy in itself.

In healing it is important to live in the now. Our past is the road traveled to get to this point and will weigh too heavy on us if we chose to carry it around. We must consolidate all that we learned from the past and let the rest go. Likewise we cannot afford to be caught up in the uncertainty of tomorrow; we must make the best of the present day and focus all our energy in our NOW otherwise we are missing the moment.

Allowing the Higher Power, the Supreme Surgeon, into our lives is crucial also in order to restore health back to the heart. He will lighten our load as we stumble to balance our intellect with our emotions. The doctor can only help when the patient tells the doctor everything. In the same way, if we do not give our full and honest account, the Surgeon cannot help us.

Sometimes we build barriers around our hearts, to protect ourselves from more pain and hurt, but in doing so we cut ourselves off from receiving love, the greatest medicine.

Finally, the passage of time is itself a healer. We must be patient with ourselves. Wounds take time to heal, but they do heal. One day the scars will remind us of the courage and strength we had at the time of need.

IT'S TIME... To have the courage (cour = heart) to open our hearts to love and healing. Have the courage to let go of the hurt and pain. Give the love you have been waiting for to others first and it will surely come back to you, multiplied. As we heal our heart and become whole again, we become agents to heal the world.

Staying Clear of Gossip

Is the need to gossip truly a need or a want? What purpose does gossiping serve the soul? Could it be that I am not happy with my own story (quite insecure, actually) and need to live someone else's by gossiping about them.

Though gossip may start out based on fact, the facts evaporate very quickly. In fact, the amount of waste thoughts, peaceless-ness and depression that results from gossip costs lives, break-ups in families, as well as thousands of dollars to corporations.

Ever tried playing Chinese Whispers? The initial message sent out is never the same that returns. For example: *Kevin Shortbread shed twenty kilos* becomes *Karin Crumble is pregnant... again!* In the space of a few minutes you see the birth of a juicy gossip. Be dubious when someone repeats a little nugget of information they've just overheard, such as: '*The Boss feels you are too slow;*' or '*Did you know that no one really likes your cooking?!*'; or '*Everyone thinks you need to use a deodorant.*' Who are no one and everyone?

Be cautious of second (or third!) hand news also. If you have not heard it yourself, you do not know HOW it was said and in WHAT context. Where possible, get the real story from the 'horse's mouth' before you take action.

Gossip spreads faster than the wind. Gossip is so powerful, that it has been known to create the down-fall of many a great kings and their kingdoms. So dangerous is this habit that it destroys the one who begins it and the accomplices who spread it. Gossip is karmic also for as one talks about others, they are being talked about in the same vein.

IT'S TIME... to put away the spice box! Don't entertain gossip and don't embellish what you hear before serving it to others. Pay no attention to hearsay and remember what others think about you is none of your business. Create a constructive wave of positive dialogues. And if you really do NEED to chinwag then praise and honour others, applaud their efforts and achievements for what goes around comes around!

Don't Take Sorrow and Don't Give Sorrow

How many of us take and give sorrow without even knowing it? We may easily understand when we give sorrow, but do we realise we are also taking the sorrow by getting upset or disheartened or complaining about trivial matters. Do we understand that in any situation we have a choice as to the feelings we create and so sorrow is not forced onto us, it is something we choose to indulge in.

Sorrow is anything that causes discomfort – it is a suffering on an emotional level; quite different from pain which is a physical state. What we call emotional pain is in fact us taking sorrow from the situation. It's not real; it's a creation of our own mind. For example, a patient could be in pain and bearing it with fortitude and yet not experiencing sorrow. Some people on a spiritual path have learnt the art of remaining in happiness even though they may be in physical pain. How is it possible you may ask!

Pain is a message from the body that comes to tell you there is something you need to change. For example, eating too much chilli food can cause ulcers; sitting too much may cause back pain; worrying too much can cause headaches, etc! Thus a physical cause results in a physical reaction.

But on the other hand to take sorrow, and then to suffer emotionally is our choice; a choice we make with our mind and intellect. Sorrow is the outcome of our interpretation of events. For example, we didn't pass the job interview and we got disheartened. Our loved one didn't call us (within 24hrs) and we think they don't love us any more. We weren't invited to a meeting or a party and we sulk.

Events are just events, they do not conspire against us, but sometimes we just put our own spin on them. Sometimes life just happens that way. Maybe we had a great CV and they admired us, but we were just not the right person for that job – in which case would we really be happy in a job that was not a good fit for us!? Perhaps our loved one was just very busy and caught up, they had no intention to hurt us through their silence. Perhaps the others thought of our best interests and knew the meeting would be a waste of our time and therefore didn't invite us!

We take a lot of sorrow from these situations when we take them personally. In fact we are projecting our needs into the situation or the person. We all want to be wanted, loved and well thought of at all times, and if there seems to be a threat against this cherished notion, sorrow and sadness kick in as our defense mechanism. This closes up our heart and once our heart is closed we can no longer flow with love, good wishes and blessings.

We may believe that we are punishing the other party and denying them of our love, kindness and inner beauty, but in actuality we are hurting ourselves more. It is the block in our heart that is causing *us* the grief, not them! In that moment, we do not act from our higher self, only the lower self, which is needy and greedy. Our higher self gives without wanting a return and our heart flows easily and constantly.

When we give sorrow to others we are creating karma for ourselves. And intense karma of this kind never rewards us with happiness, only further sorrow. There are many ways in which we give subtle sorrow. Here are a couple of examples.

For example, I may have wealth and that is my good fortune but to flaunt it in front of a person who has nothing, that is intentionally creating sorrow. On the other side, if I envy someone because they have the latest gizmos (and remember… because of their good fortune) then that is my problem! Instead of taking sorrow from everything let me see what I do have and take happiness from that. Never judge a book by its cover.

Also, by looking at the defects and faults of others I am giving sorrow; in that moment, I am not uplifting the other. In spiritual language, I am only 'kicking' the other person more. They have 'fallen' because of their shortcoming and yet I am making them weaker by focusing on their imperfections.

I have to build such immunity to the sorrow that not only am I able to tolerate the sorrow, but turn it around to my favour. If I have the strength of virtues such as contentment, self respect and self worth, to name a few, then I have a higher threshold or immunity to sorrow and suffering in my life. I am then able to deflect the criticisms of others, rather than immediately having feelings of hurt, rejection or self-pity.

Ultimately I create more sorrow from the sorrow by exaggerating the situation and enlarging it with my waste thoughts. Learn to give others the benefit of the doubt. Remain positive as much as you can; there is always benefit behind everything, even if you can't see it just yet!

IT'S TIME... to stop giving and taking sorrow and to use spiritual wisdom to take the best from the situation. Sorrow is created as the result of my own thinking and so choose to have self-respect and a heart that is flowing. Don't take things too personally. See things more clearly, without the clouds of emotion, and you will be able to respond appropriately. Then you will see that a life of happiness is possible... always!

Thoughts Become Things

A person who knows the power of his words will be very cautious to choose his words carefully. There is a saying that 'thoughts become things', and this can certainly become true if the thoughts or words are uttered with deep conviction.

If one truly believes they will always get ahead in life, they will make it happen, because they have set up the law in their mind for it to happen. If another believes they are a hopeless case, then that will result. Either way, they are right! As each one affirms certain beliefs, their thoughts, words and actions will be in alignment with the belief, and this in turn will influence the course of their life and destiny.

Take, for example, HM Queen Rania of Jordan who was born to a middle class family in Kuwait. A chance outing with a new co-worker to a dinner party hosted by Prince Abdullah's sister changed her life forever. When their eyes met across the room, it was love at first sight and the Prince married her just five months later. What are the chances that you are given the name Rania (queen) at birth and you actually become one!

Gandhi held a vision of an India free from the British Raj. His vision became a reality through his unswerving conviction that success could be achieved through the method of *'satyagraha'*, loosely translated as insistence on truth, and *'ahimsa'*, non violence.

When singer Celine Dion was 18 years of age, she saw Michael Jackson performing on television and told her manager that she wanted to be a superstar like him! During her

 It's Time... to Change

spectacular career Celine has been honored with over a 1000 awards and World Music Awards recognized her status as the best-selling female artist of all time.

There are several other examples of such people who have made things happen simply by the power of their belief and the determination that it brings. Words and affirmations are powerful, but belief is the fuel that guarantees success.

As we repeat certain thoughts and words, we are endorsing them. In fact, there is a whole science around names and how each letter and syllable emits a vibration that affects us subtly every time our name is used.

It is not just a case of repeating certain words over and again (for example: 'I am the perfect weight for me!') and hoping that something good will happen! We have to actually believe the affirmation to be true. Often we are unconsciously affirming the negative. How many times do we think about what we don't want to happen, only to find it becoming a reality? We wonder why we have all the bad luck – not realising that it could, in fact, be our creation!

This is why it is so important to make sure that our thoughts about ourselves and others are positive because our thoughts create a certain vibration that inevitably affect our minds, our bodies and the people and environment around us. For example we each have the power to 'think ourselves sick' or create good health according to our thoughts or what we believe to be true, but sometimes we do not give importance to our 'ordinary' thoughts, or realize what they are doing to us! We don't recognize their potency and so we just let them continue to pass.

Prayers are positive affirmations. A prayer is an elevated thought, intention or vision. They are a form of communication with God, and therefore, when done with deep faith and conviction, create a very elevated vibration and feeling. Chants, mantras, carols and hymns also instill an elevated harmonic feeling. The words or statements have been carefully crafted to vibrate at a certain frequency.

If we believe that every word carries a vibration, then it holds true that certain words weigh more in energy than others. Thus it is important to 'weigh' our words before releasing them. For once they are 'out there' there is no way to get them back – we have already informed the universe of our intention! Cheap, nasty and dirty words always carry a negative vibration and create a heavy, negative feeling both in the person emitting it and the one receiving it. Imagine the toxicity of the mind that creates such low thoughts and words. Thus it is so important to check our thoughts for they will soon become our words and our actions.

For example, 'Om' or 'Aum' is the monarch of all mantras and chanting it can be very beneficial. Thought by some to be the original sound of the universe, it cleanses the mind, controls emotions and balances the chakras in the body. It relaxes physically, mentally and emotionally and charges the surrounding atmosphere.

Meditation and contemplation on positive virtues or values are also forms of affirmation. In Raja Yoga Meditation one is acknowledging one's true identity as a peaceful, loveful, powerful being. Affirming what we know to be true by experiencing it in our meditation, quickly makes it become a clear reality in our everyday life.

Get clear on exactly what you want, and focus on that, don't just affirm what you don't want. Meditate on it on a daily basis. Let God know, let the universe know, start believing in it, start living it as if it has already happened. And then watch your future unfold.

IT'S TIME... to affirm only the best for you. Be selective about your thoughts because they are soon to become your reality. Create only positive thoughts, words and actions, that you want

It's Time... to Change

to see take fruit because once you have 'made your order' the universe will surely deliver. With every positive vibrational note we create in our life, we create a beautiful symphony!

Minding Our Language

So often do we find ourselves using negative, derogatory and defamatory language that does not serve our spirit, and on the contrary fails to honour our soul? The way that we speak to ourselves, what we can call our 'self talk' has an affect on our lives and the lives of others. At a physical level negative language rocks the immune system of our body. As we consistently use disparaging language, we are in actual fact invoking and reinforcing the very things we dislike in our lives.

For example, a friend who constantly kept saying that she needed a break, soon ended up with a broken leg after falling from a ladder while trying to organize her closet. She finally got the time to 'put up her feet' and have a good rest for three months! Not quite the break she had in mind.

Another student who kept repeating: 'I can't see what the problem is…' experienced colour blindness!

How often do we find ourselves saying that so and so is a 'pain in the neck', and then realize that we too have developed a pain in our neck and shoulders! We have taken on their problem and made it ours. When we insist on holding this negative vision of them, then the very thing that we are focusing on become ours!

As we use repetitive language referring to pain, we hope to gain some attention and sympathy from others. In fact, the more we think about and verbalise our pain, the more it increases! And this habit is reinforced to such a degree that even when there is no pain, we play out the part of the 'poor me', in the hope of getting some attention and devotion from others!

It's Time... to Change

The use of language such as 'Silly me', 'I can't seem to get anything right', 'How stupid of me', 'Nothing works around here...' does not serve to make us better people and only makes matters worse in our lives.

Repetitive negative thinking also makes our fears come true. Whatever we think about will be our creation, so we have to pay attention to what we are constantly invoking. Likewise, whatever I resist, persists, so they say. Therefore, if I attempt to push someone or something away…it will only push back!

Minding Our Language

There is a saying which goes something like, 'be careful of what you wish for, because you will surely receive it.' How conscious are we of what we want and truly desire? If everyone in the world focused on spiritual peace and love instead of focusing on the negative and unwholesome things in life such as blaming, condemning, and therefore giving energy to the 'outlaws' of society, then the world would be very different.

I truly believe we can create a world of peace together once we focus our mind on the good, the positive and that which will be healing for myself, others and the planet. When we hold these types of thoughts in our minds and have a positive vision for the world, then the world will become a beautiful place in which to live.

IT'S TIME ... for us to become mindful of the language we use towards ourselves, others and the world. Because every thought is energy, and when we become careless with our thoughts we forget that there will always be an effect somewhere in the universe. The time and date may be unspecified, but the law of energy states that... whatever we put out in the universe... must come back... at some point... in some way!

Less is More

The term 'minimalist' is often used in architecture or design to describe something which is stripped to its bare, but well-crafted essentials. The term 'Less is More' elegantly describes this sophisticated and thoughtful approach to living simply. As much as we may appreciate the beauty of this type of simplicity in our surroundings, do we appreciate the value of our thoughts in the same way? Are we just as industrious in creating simple but elegant thoughts? Too few of us give value to this wonderful personal challenge, perhaps because it seems difficult to accomplish and, being a very subtle accomplishment, is less easy for others to admire.

Any designer will tell you that it takes far greater precision and effort to create something apparently simple. To indiscriminately fill every corner of our home with objects of different sizes, colours, shapes and textures is easy to do, but it would not result in a relaxing atmosphere. To create a pleasant ambient space, the objects need to be carefully selected, each one adding to the overall harmony.

The same goes for our inner, mental and metaphysical domain. Are our thoughts overcrowding our mind, each one vying for attention? Or are we careful to create only the thoughts that will bring harmony and space to the soul? For space brings to mind freedom – no walls, borders, boundaries, just an open horizon and unlimited possibilities; no wonder many of us aspire to live in front of an ocean, a lake or an open vista.

If less is more, then how much do we really need? How much is enough? We may own 100 pairs of shoes, but we can still only wear one pair at a time. And will we ever be satisfied with the amount we earn? Probably not, that is, at least not until we are satisfied with ourselves.

Raja Yoga Meditation is the mastery over the mind; meaning to practise living with less and less clutter, which in turn brings more and more peace of mind. If you have managed to convince your mind with living with 'less' then nothing else really matters, i.e. no public opinion will affect you. The purpose is not to stop, suppress or force your thoughts into an ascetic lifestyle, but rather to gently let go of the unnecessary and by doing so give yourself space to breathe and 'be yourself'.

In our fast-paced world this suggestion might seem outpaced by reality, but our greatest thinkers, creators, artists and athletes knew its value in their pursuit of perfection. Simplicity brings clarity and focus into our lives, which in turn opens doors for solutions to enter into our consciousness. With focus, we make inner space, where others struggle to breathe.

IT'S TIME... to check your greatest energy source, your thoughts. Pause to give yourself space. Assign rarity value to your thoughts by choosing only those of the highest quality. Refuse to give room to clutter or inessential mental 'furniture'. Create moments of space for yourself and allow your creativity to emerge – the renovation in the interior décor of your mind will mean fewer thoughts giving birth to more peace and happiness.

Making an Appointment with Yourself

We can be very good at creating schedules and making appointments with others to better organize our lives... yet when was the last time you actually made an appointment with yourself to be with your self and to better organize your mind, thoughts, beliefs, attitudes, emotions, feelings and all those subtle factors that govern your responses and reactions to life?

Making time for the self is healthy and allows you to regain your balance and rejuvenate your energy, so that when you step back into the world, the family or the team, you are able to be your self and give more of yourself.

As you give yourself permission for this, you will begin to realize that in taking out an hour for yourself there is tremendous benefit for the self and that you are able to give back quality time, appreciation and attention. It also allows for the creativity to flourish, thoughts to spring easily and naturally rather than through force, slows and calms the breath, lowers the stress levels and allows for a clearer decision making process.

Spending time with 'The Self' means exactly that: watching TV, interacting on Facebook, playing video games, shopping or reading magazines do not count as spending time alone, it just means that you have exchanged one world of noise and distraction for another one! There is little benefit in that.

It is an act of Mother Nature that every organism needs time to replenish, refill, and renew – without it the species perishes. In the same way, what will I be able to give others if I am empty inside? Often, when I am feeling frustrated, annoyed or irritated at people and situations, it is not because the other party is the problem, but because I am not getting my own needs met in that I am not having ample sleep, rest, space and quiet time. Often it's a sign of unease within my own self.

Spending time alone is not frightening, as some people think, nor is it a waste of time, or a reason to feel guilty. To spend time in solitude walking, thinking, and getting to know one's own mind, thoughts and emotions is actually incredibly healing.

If silence and solitude are scary to us it is because we don't know ourselves. Just as in some relationships, we find the people we don't know quite scary. But once we discover their beautiful facets it's another story.

In fact, sometimes we don't want to keep our own company because, truth be known, we don't really like ourselves very much and so we avoid ourselves by engaging in the company of others! However, the more I get to know me, the more I can get to like myself. If I look for the treasures that are deep inside instead of seeing faults, criticizing, beating myself up, then I may just make a new friend! Then the journey of acceptance, forgiveness and self-appreciation can begin.

Time is such a commodity that it can easily get sucked up by those around you, unless you consciously decide to slot in a time for your own self! When was the last time you actually enjoyed your own company without the dependency of another?

Decide that you will spend time with yourself each day to get to know yourself. And that once a week you will treat yourself to something special. Perhaps a meal by yourself ... and instead of talking and just passing the food down, enjoy every morsel you eat (hopefully it will be vegetarian!). Or, take a long walk and just allow yourself to absorb every detail of the

It's Time... to Change

scenery, as though you are seeing it for the first time. Take time to journal your thoughts, write an article, a poem or a song. Sit in silence and watch the sun come up and enjoy the wonder of nature and the wonder of your own self. Meditate on your innate qualities of peace, love and truth and learn to just BE.

IT'S TIME ... to respect and appreciate yourself by taking out quality time for yourself. You will become stronger, happier, better, more thoughtful, more loving and a more interesting person to be with. It is in fact one of the greatest gifts you can give to yourself. Rumi, the Sufi poet once said something to this effect ... the more you get to know yourself, the more you will become a lover of thyself!

Sulk Not – Smile a Lot

Sulking is a habit we learn from early on in our childhood and which most of us carry into adulthood. Sulking is only the top layer of many layers of resentment – beneath it are many unmet needs that need to be explored. How does one deal with this noxious habit?

Sulking is a silent protest. It is a form of anger. It's our subtle way of saying I am not happy, and I am upset with you (or the situation). Anger is a secondary emotion, beneath it are many unmet needs and the 'sulker' is implying, by you ignoring me, you or the drama of life are not meeting my needs!

The word 'sullen' and 'sulk,' originate from *sullein*, which means alone. When we are sullen, we are actually feeling very alone. The world is a place where I perceive that no one actually loves or understands me.

Just as children cry and sulk when they don't get their choice of candy or preferred toy, we as adults also do the same when we don't get what we want. It's actually a cry to want to be loved, understood, included, involved, integrated, and embraced. When this doesn't happen, we feel helpless, abandoned and alone – very much like the child who couldn't get his way.

Sulkers use their silence as a means of emotional deployment. Since they are unable to control the situation actively through their strength of self-worth, they try to gain power by manipulating others through guilt and blame. From their ego-centric perspective friends and family try everything to 'make me happy' and I will be the centre of attention. And as they do, I *will* have gotten my way! Just like the child who threw the temper tantrum and eventually got his mother's cuddles and loving affection.

Whenever we have little self-worth we will always try to gain control of situations or people through manipulative means. After all, sulking gets us some attention and makes us feel powerful, it gets us noticed – and who would want to voluntarily give up that power. Stopping sulking involves working with issues of self-worth and building an inner resolve.

Sulking is in fact immature, or in other words, it's the inner child within us that has not quite developed yet. It's a feeble way of addressing situations, not a courageous one. We replicate the same behavioural patterns of our childhood and why not – they seem to work and get us the same results – but do they?! We *can* continue with the old and familiar patterns, but it does not make us strong in our ability to face situations; in our communications skills; it does not give us the strength to move on and to take charge of our life; or take blessings from others – we are forever dependent on others to fix us or our situation.

Sulking keeps us selfish – it's an inverted ego. It's all about 'me' and how I can manipulate the situation in my favour. Because we don't get our way, we don't want others to get theirs either! We play the game of 'One-upmanship' by intimidating others with our wants and needs.

And in the long run, we don't win friends. We only perpetuate distance in relationships. That is why people prefer not to deal with sulkers – they are over-sensitive, self absorbed and arrogant. The other party has to go to great lengths to pay attention and not upset the sulker!

Long-term sulking is unhealthy and toxic for the mind and body. Sulking is a state of mind – a mood you create and remain buried in. You continue to create negative thoughts and are convinced there is a conspiracy against you. Repetitive sulky moods are self-destructive.

Increase self-worth. Create a pedigree of your own – so what if someone doesn't invite you to the party – organize your own party! Create a league of your own. Boost your feelings and thoughts of self worth – only then will others respect you and your preferences. Learn to express your feelings truthfully, calmly and openly whilst respecting yourself and the other party.

Create more honest relationships based on connectedness and trust. Stop playing the game of making the other party guess all the time. As you reach out with your love, forgive and communicate clearly, you will open doors and invite others in, defusing isolation and alone-ness.

IT'S TIME... to stop sulking and to start smiling at life. Build an inner self respect and don't fret over situations. Be mature and communicate your needs clearly. Know that the universe loves you and is working to make you stronger and more powerful – from the inside out. Always stay in a party mood, happy and light, and you will be surrounded by love, so much so, that you will never feel alone.

Back to Basics

The meltdown of the world's financial sytems in the first decade of the twenty-first century has heralded years of austerity for many around the globe. Governments, companies, and most probably you and me, are cutting back to make ends meet, or at least to make things go further!

In a world where consumerism is getting increasingly crazy – the word 'unsustainable' was surpassed a long time ago – is it such a bad thing to consider getting 'back to basics'?

Most youngsters nowadays have grown up in a disposable culture – a world where things don't wear out, they just get dumped to be replaced with the newest and latest. They probably have never heard of the term darning a sock or fixing a kite; they just get replaced with new ones. In the 'old days' it used to be fun saving up for something. There was a greater satisfaction of having 'earned' the object of our desire.

I recall my own camping experiences as a youngster – living with the bare essentials, sleeping under the starry sky with Mother Earth as my bed. Learning to live with little is not just a luxury but also a necessity. Planet earth is being depleted of its resources – let us do what we can to help. For example, utilize less tissues, napkins and toilet rolls! Reduce, re-use, re-cycle, re-turn, repair and so on, wherever possible.

We need to simplify our lives. As we reduce the clutter in our mind, we will automatically reduce the clutter in the attic, basement and garage! Curtailing our desires is the first step towards living simply.

Declutter your wardrobe. Whatever clothes you have not worn in the last year or more need to be given away. Storing old clothes and shoes is like old energy, it does not give room to the new to live and breathe.

Cut back on greasy and fast foods before poor health forces you to. Eating oily and sugary and over processed foods may seem tasty now but will leave you feeling bitter when you have to take the pills to solve the ills. Eating wholesome, nutritious – mostly raw – food is part of good health, but so is eating less; we need less food than we actually think we do. Most of the time, we eat to feed the emotion rather than the appetite. Eating well will create a healthy happy mood.

Relationships also, are all too disposable in today's world – or so it seems. This may sound strange, but what about getting back to basics in the area of our relationships? Do we hold on to certain relationships for the wrong reasons? Back to basics means examining what relationships are for... trust, love, and honesty... going beyond the superficial, the pretty packaging and the bows and ribbons in our relationships and getting REAL.

Don't hold on to people out of obligation or compulsion. Trust and engage, but do so with love. If there is a relationship that seems to be sapping your energy or weakening your spirit, then think twice about how much time you are giving to that relationship. As a meditator we will eventually be able to get on with everyone, but only after we have built immunity.

All our cyber relationships on the social media platforms are built upon electricity and once that 'plug' is pulled we will be left feeling isolated and lonely. It is better to build an inner resolve and begin building a relationship with the self.

Simplify your vision. Getting back to basics means not to see others with a heavy set of expectations. When we have expectations of others we actually complicate our lives further. Unfulfilled expectations lead to resentment in relationships. If we simply accepted each soul with love and compassion, then they would more likely live up to our expectations (if we had any!).

When you next go shopping, simplify your list by asking this question: 'What do I need and what do I want?' Further question the 'I need' list and you should be able to reduce it by half. In the process of trying to simplify our life, we accumulate gadgets and appliances that we don't really know how to use or take care of, and so at the end of the day we have collected a heap of plastic.

Sometimes we hoard stuff out of fear – it makes us feel secure. But then we create a false reality for ourselves. There is no protection within these walls or applications, only in virtue. I need to live by a set of values that are freeing and uplifting. Real security comes from knowing who I am – without any external dependencies.

Let me also simplify my conversations. A lot of people have the habit of repeating what they have already just shared, or talk aloud their thoughts to get clarity. Wouldn't it be better to get it clear in our own heads first, instead of filling other people's heads with our garbage? Getting back to basics in our conversations allows the silence to be the backdrop. Silence speaks volumes – if we care to listen.

Perhaps the most life-changing aspect of back to basics is when I understand and realise who I am spiritually. I am not just a human body, my body is an instrument, a costume, a vehicle of expression. But it is not 'I'. I am a soul, energy, a spark, an eternal, indestructible being. I am just a tiny dot of light!

IT'S TIME... to get back to basics and get to the heart of what really matters. Why hoard things for a rainy day when someone else can be making use of them today. Try to live without your mobile phone for a day or abstain from looking at the computer and your emails and see if you can manage, without feeling a vacuum. Look around your house and see what you can reduce and recycle. Declutter your spaces – make room for newness. Take moments of quiet and silence and get in touch with nature, the inner and the outer – you will be more at peace knowing, you have done all you could to cooperate with Mother Earth.

Think Less, Do More

How many times have you found yourself procrastinating, when the job would only take you a few moments, minutes or hours to complete if you attended to it? Do you find yourself thinking a lot and as a result end up doing less? If so, then read on...

One of our greatest assets is our thoughts. How much do we use that asset throughout the day without even 'thinking' about it! Do we stop to count? Imagine, if each time we created a thought, we were spending dollars or dinars (you can decide the amount per thought) – we would certainly stop to think about what we were thinking, right?!

Dadi Janki, the head of Brahma Kumaris, said it's not just a question of thinking less, but of not thinking at all! Meaning, we need to learn to silence the mind; to create only the right thought for each action.

Yes, imagine a time, or a world, in which we only think that which we want to give life to. Imagine also, if everything we thought of came to life – it would be pretty embarrassing at times wouldn't it?

Just because people can't see your negative thoughts doesn't mean you get away with the crime. Negative thoughts drain the mind and body of energy. Negativity is a hole that creates leakage, draining the soul of its invaluable power. Power that took time to accumulate! We wonder why we are so pooped by the end of the day! Could it be that we allow our minds too long a leash?

There is a story of two monks who were walking from one village to another. Their vow of chastity also meant they were not allowed to touch any woman. Along the way they saw a young woman afraid to cross the river alone. The elder monk picked her up gently and walked across with her. After dropping her on the other side, the two monks continued their journey in silence. After about two hours the younger monk could no longer conceal his concern and asked the older monk why he had broken the vow and touched a woman. To which the older monk replied, 'I picked her up two hours ago and dropped her there and then, but it seems you have been carrying her all this time!'

Repetitive thinking also depletes the soul of energy. Ask yourself, why you would revisit a thought recurrently? Primarily because you are unsure, or take it a step further, maybe because you are insecure. It may not be a bad thing to re-check a thought once or twice for sake of clarity, but if you are constantly unclear, always confused, and riddled with self-doubt then you need to take a deeper look at yourself. Learn to decide, take risks and then flow with the drama of life. It's more fun!

When you think less and decide more, you will accomplish a lot more. The amount of time it takes to iron a few shirts or wash a few dishes is a few minutes compared to the hours you may deliberate over it... so as in Nike© style, 'Just do it'!

You will begin to feel more productive and enjoy more efficiency in your life. This will give you a sense of accomplishment and hence more satisfaction.

Remember, life is not all about getting there, or achieving more of this and that... it's about being. Learn to be. Learn to master your inner state and the outer state will follow suit. If the mind is clear and the heart is clean, this will reflect in your surroundings and relationships. Learn to feel every thought before immediately acting upon it.

It's Time... to Change

Between every stimulus and response, there is a space... a space in which to choose. Choose to be calm, choose to be at peace, choose to be still, and choose to be silent....

IT'S TIME... to think less and to BE more! Be selective about the thoughts you create – waste and negative deplete you of your soul power. Learn to value your treasure of thoughts – after all it is powerful thinkers who become powerful do'ers! Make a decision with conviction, then the question of 'to be or not to be', will not arise!

Spiritual Warrior

Often the picture of a warrior conjures up images of a battered and wounded soldier, breathless and exasperated! The image of a spiritual warrior is somewhat different.

A spiritual warrior is always ready and prepared to meet any challenge with alacrity. They have no fear, just love and lightness. Spiritual warriors are balanced – grounded and firm. They never tire because they never get wounded. Unlike the other warrior, this one smiles in the face of uncertainty!

The spiritual warrior walks with a pride and confidence – even before he begins, he knows victory is guaranteed. No task is too great or prodigious because he has cultivated such inner self-respect and a big open heart that is willing and generous.

He is never distracted or side tracked, lazy or careless. He cannot even indulge in vanity, for the warrior knows that to lose focus for even a moment would allow the enemy to gain ground!

Spiritual warriors are brave and courageous. They keep themselves protected with the shield or aura of God's light. Their feet hardly touch the ground and their 'artillery' is always on hand.

The weapons of a spiritual warrior are not the usual ones made of stone or wood or gunpowder. They flex the muscles of their mind with the inner powers – the power to face, to adjust, to discern, to withdraw, to cooperate, to let go and move on when necessary. They also ensure they are full of inner beauty: lightness, kindness, generosity, humility, benevolence, compassion, beauty and more. And most of all they carry the 'weapons' of love, peace, truth, bliss and purity. These tools need sharpening from time to time through meditation.

Spiritual warriors are known to go through 'spiritual deaths'. One such death is ego, another is attachment. Learning to 'die' is a given on the spiritual journey; in fact it is when we have truly died that we can really awaken and live. Therefore the battle is not with the enemy out there, but with the one within. Once I have 'killed' or, for sake of semantics, transformed myself, metamorphosed myself, then there is no battle left to fight. For example, if you don't have an ego, then no one can dent or crush your ego. If there is no attachment, then no one can give you pain!

This is illustrated well in the Bhagavad Gita. The whole Gita is a dialogue between Lord Krishna and Arjuna, the greatest archer ever. They are standing in the middle of a huge battlefield and Arjuna, having won the first choice, chooses to have Lord Krishna by his side and his rival cousin Duroydhana has accepted what would have been his first choice anyway, the whole army.

Arjuna seeing that his enemies are his relatives and loved ones, becomes weak-kneed and refuses to fight! It is then that Lord Krishna begins by giving him knowledge and inspiration of various kinds. One of the last significant statements that are very moving is when Lord Krishna explains, 'Whether you kill them in your mind or on the battlefield, it is the same thing.' Lord Krishna was urging him to fight not the violent battle, but the internal one of the web of attachment.

Some attachments can be so severe that they take on the form of a 'vein'. The vein channels the blood, the life force, from one organ to another. In the same manner the 'blood of attachment' affects all those to whom you are attached. If something happens to you, it is as though it is happening to them, such is the influence of the attachment. And vice versa is true, if something is happening to them it feels as though its happening to you.

Arjuna was a spiritual warrior. The very meaning of his name is the one who cannot be defeated. We are all being called on to be Arjuna, spiritual warriors who are not defeated by life's trivial games.

Having conquered our attachment to people, money and possessions, food and taste buds, clothes and comforts, our final battle will be with our attachment and identification with our body. The 'departure' needs to be so smooth and natural, as familiar as a mini-meditation. The feeling is of moving from one floor to another – from this worldly plane to another. No tug of war, no pull of the body, people or comforts and absolutely no pain – the soul simply flies on.

Meditation is in fact like a mini death. We learn to separate from the consciousness of this body and fly beyond to our Home of Light. The more we practice this, the more in fact, our 'battles' will reduce!

IT'S TIME... to look within and seek out the enemy. The spiritual warrior blames nobody, and takes full responsibility for the self and the battlefield he has found himself in. Cut those veins of attachment that drain so much energy from the soul, kill the ego, become light and most of all learn to smile because you are that Arjuna and victory is guaranteed!

Student Life is the Best

On a spiritual path, it is imperative that the yogi (one who meditates) sustains an attitude of learning at all times. Once he (or she) thinks he has learnt everything, his learning stops and he would not only go backwards but maybe even return further back from the starting point as he has now given birth to a new ego. Reminding oneself that life itself offers the best schooling and to always remain open to the learning, keeps one light, easy and humble.

Discipline
One of the first principles of student life is the discipline. If I am unable to attend school every day I will miss out on the assortment and depth of education provided, which will only lead to failure at the end of the year. On the spiritual path it is also important to study on a daily basis. Going to Church on Sundays only for an hour or the Mosque on Fridays will not redeem the devotee of all his sins, nor provide the strength to deal with life's increasing daily challenges.

Just as we provide food for the body every day, three times a day (and some maybe in between also!), it is crucial that we feed the soul with positive and powerful thoughts frequently. Disciplining the mind disciplines the life; there is clarity and precision. Be determined every morning to begin your day with a dose of spiritual wisdom. And be strict about not allowing your thoughts to be distracted toward the negative!

Disciplines create a system in our life and the systems are in place so that we need not think further. This should not mean we become thoughtless in the sense of becoming robotic, but rather it gives a break to the mind (thoughts) and to the intellect (the decision maker). Disciplines create a smooth rhythm to my life that helps me conserve my energy for more useful thought processes. If I break that tempo, there is a price to pay. Perhaps I will lose my peace or my happiness and then I will have to work harder at creating the flow again, like the student who misses class and then has to work additional hours to catch up.

Punctuality and Attendance
Sometimes, the student may not be so bright, but he will secure extra marks for punctuality and attendance. His commitment, will and determination very often melt the heart of the teacher. And even if the student is bright, regular attendance will guarantee that he has caught everything he could have to pass the final paper.

It goes without saying that on this journey it is so important to study punctually and daily. The best time is the early morning hours when the mind is fresh and can engage easily. If I miss this precious part of the day, then I will be 'late'! In order to regain my inner silence and stillness I will then have to compete with the noisy world around me that is scurrying to begin its day.

Homework
Student life is incomplete without 'homework'; this is the work you do at home, alone, on your own. Taking time to be in solitude and to revise spiritual concepts is very important. Without this positive input the mind will find something else to regurgitate. Revising spiritual principles in solitude will coagulate them in the soul. They will become embedded in your memory track for you to be able to retrieve later when you need them.

Examinations and Tests

Students are tested from time to time to examine how well they are doing in school. Life presents many tests throughout the day and examinations throughout our lifetime, but it's up to me to see them as a block and 'stop learning' or an opportunity to claiming a 'masters degree in life'!

The reason why this spiritual path is a high one is because the yogi has to pass at every second. He can't afford to allow one single, small, negative thought to creep in, for it will ferment and breed quickly, wrecking all that has been built till now.

Our spiritual assignment on a daily basis is to maintain our peace and cool. There will be many things that will come our way to shake us off this seat of stability. But the firm yogi does not wobble.

Just as the student who is determined to pass keeps reminding himself of his victory, so too, through meditation, remind yourself that you are a peaceful being. Cultivate an attitude of gratitude, feel the abundance in your life, and think of God Almighty and how He is looking after you. These are just a few ideas of how you can preserve your peaceful day and 'pass with honors'.

Research and Experimentation

A good student does his research and enquiry in the subject. In fact, it is blind faith to simply listen and follow. In the same way go forth and experiment with these spiritual truths, explore them and discover them for yourself. Try out different ideas every week by picking a different theme of effort such as exercising silence or contentment or positivity. You may wish to remind yourself using sticky notes and see how you fare. Once you speak with the authority of experience then no one will be able to refute you!

Free Education

Like all good things in life this spiritual education is free of charge. If you can stay open to the learning, then you are being educated, enlightened and awoken to your inner truth. If you resist the tests will persist; if you snooze you will lose. If you can accept and embrace then you will learn the gentle art of detachment and discover that lifelong student life is the best.

IT'S TIME... to go back to being a good student! Ensure that there is an intake of spiritual wisdom in your life daily and study punctually every morning. Thank every test that comes, for it only informs you of how much more inner work that needs to be done. Apply some disciplines to your life; you will thank them also for the time you will save otherwise. Prepare yourself for your 'final paper' – your 'highest degree', the destiny that is in your hands of purifying your heart and your soul. And you will become part of God's Honor Roll.

Imagery

One of the powerful techniques we use in meditation is the ability to visualize. Nature provides many examples of how we can ebb and flow with the various energies of life. As we sit with these mental images in meditation they become imprinted in our memory like real life events. The mind carries a recording of these images and at times calls upon them, for better or for worse! Hence it is so important that we filter the images which we want to carry in the suitcase of the soul.

Let's try the following exercise…
Imagine you are a tree… the roots representing the various belief systems you have adopted from childhood, which go deep and define your present identity. If the roots are strong, you are confident and proud of your accomplishments. For those who feel the foundation to be a little weak, there is hope: simply add a drop of pure and powerful consciousness to the soul on a daily basis. Consciousness is created with a stream of thoughts; the more powerful the thoughts, the more powerful the consciousness and therefore your spiritual root system.

The trunk, the torso, a single piece of wood, is solid and strong, undivided and immovable. One means single, no duality and hence no conflict (duality gives birth to conflict). Thus the trunk represents the most stable part of you, the knowledge that you are a spiritual being; there is no doubt and no hesitation. No one can refute this truth. This wisdom makes you secure and solid, because although the elements of matter may change, I the being am eternal.

Imagery

As with every living object in the world, for it to survive and function, apart from solidity it also requires the suppleness to yield. The branches of the tree are the lithe part, able to sway and swing with the wind; it is with this ability to yield and to bend that the trunk remains protected.

Now imagine that you (the tree still!) are standing in front of the sun – sunbathing! The rays of the 'Supreme Sun' heal and nourish the self. The Sun's rays are like a laser beam, burning away the impurities. And as I the soul 'sun tan' in front of the rays of that Supreme Light, I am being coloured by His virtues and powers!

As you stand tall in the meadow of life, balance the art of steadfastness and adaptation. If you are stiff and arrogant, you will be knocked down easily by life's currents. Like the example of a tree, the more it matures, the more it is able to provide a place of rest and comfort to the tired traveler. It is with this capacity to flow that you are able to protect and strengthen the inner being.

IT'S TIME... to experiment using different visual imagery for every meditation experience. For example, one time be a lighthouse beaming light into the world. Another time, be a mirror that reflects God's light – and your duty is to simply keep that mirror clean and clear! Be a seed, introverted and humble; potential waiting to explode; the creation of something new. Sometimes be a rock, firm and strong and sometimes be the water that softens the edges. Be the ocean, merging everyone's weaknesses. Be a bird, soaring above situations and gaining new perspective. And as you experiment... turn your face toward the 'Sun', for without the sunshine, there is no Life!

Full Stop

Putting a 'full stop' to certain life events is sometimes not so easy and we often find ourselves inserting commas and exclamation marks instead. Why is it so difficult to apply this tiny point at times and to move on?

In English grammar the full stop normally comes at the end of a sentence, to denote the end of a statement and before we start the next one: a place where one feels it's time to duly stop. In the drama of our life, if we have not arrived at this 'end' state in our mind then we will forever elongate our 'life sentence' with extra commas. And, in fact, when a sentence goes on for too long it can become cumbersome and quite impossible to grasp. So when something drags on for too long in one's life, it can become not only annoying and frustrating, but one can get stuck in the old energy of one's negativity.

The best way to enjoy a story or a good read is to have frequent stops and regular intervals. This allows us a moment to digest what has gone before and to prepare for what is to come. Understand a full stop as a start of a new thought, not merely the end of an old one. It is an opportunity to begin something anew. Look forward and not behind. Learn from the past and then let go. The only way to change the past is to create a better future.

Also, instead of commas we sometimes accentuate our life with exclamation marks: those high tones of expressions of wonderment, amazement and disbelief! However, we then get surprised and feel let down when we come across the imperfections because we had created an illusion of a perfect person or situation. Knowing that we don't live in a perfect world, and we can all be fallible, allows us to not have unreasonable expectations and stay stable in our feelings and responses.

Knowing that this whole play of life is just about a bunch of actors playing their parts together on one stage reduces the blows and shocks, and waste thoughts. Today they may be '*Superman*' and tomorrow not so super; but they are just playing their part. Condemn the act not the actor. Do not confuse the role and costume with the soul. Raja Yoga meditation teaches us that every soul in their original nature is pure and divine. Look at that originality, the soul, not the one in process on stage right now.

If putting a full stop means to apply the brakes, then faulty brakes means we are unable to stop at the right time and place. So it raises the question whether we ever maintained our brakes in the first place, or just went about our life expecting never to crash! Maintaining our mind every day with pure, positive and powerful thoughts will ensure that we don't collide and stay focused on our journey.

The final full stop is indicative of 'The End'. Where, after all, the action and thoughts move into a silent, contemplative stage. The story is over and nothing more can be added. How often throughout the day are we able to apply this full stop – not half a stop – to the various stories running in our mind, in order that we can experience peace and tranquility.

It is easier, and can take only a second, to apply a full stop in a state of complete soul consciousness. In the eternity of things, nothing material really matters. In the awareness of being a body we struggle to preserve our image by writing volumes. With the pen of our actions, we justify and embellish our ego, we seek confirmation and approval, we argue and quarrel – and the story never ends.

Full stop is about closure, not so much with the other party, as much as it is about respect for the self. If you are unable to put a full stop, then how will you begin a new chapter? Honour yourself, by putting a stop to waste thoughts and a need for further drama in your life. If you still wish to ride the roller coaster of emotions, then it will be hard for you to experience a constant high.

IT'S TIME... to put a complete full stop. Learn from the past and then let go. Take the pen of action into your own hand and begin a new chapter in your life. As new stories arise in your mind, keep them short and keep applying the brake. And when you put the final stop in your life at 'The End', your novel should be worth reading over and over again.

Dying to be Thin

In a world where physical image and ideal body shape are given more importance than values and morals, it's important to consider the consequences of living in a society that offers an idealistic and false notion of what beauty is. Too many young women (and men also for that matter) are literally dying in the pursuit of a perfect body shape. The pressure to conform or the need to be accepted is greater than their sense of self-value and self-respect. If the price they are paying is their own life, then it raises the question of whether the journey toward a slim and slender body is really worth it.

Let me state from the offset that I am not a doctor, nor am I capable of treating such disorders such as bulimia or anorexia nervosa, but what I can offer here is a discussion about the need for the afflicted person to increase their self worth and self value. It is also about the onlooker exercising more acceptance and less judgment. These so-called diseases of the modern world are simply a manifestation of the dis-ease a person feels within their own inner self. Social attitudes and media portrayals promoting skinny body types are an aspect of a culture that we are all complicit with in some way, and these also need to be reconsidered.

The power of the media is a double-edged sword. On the one hand it can educate, whilst on the other hand it can be a 'weapon of mass destruction'. There is evidence that media portrayals of an 'ideal' body image can be a contributing factor to Bulimia. A study of schoolgirls in Fiji showed that in the first three years after the introduction of television in 1995, incidents of bulimia rose from 0% to 11.3% [*http://en.wikipedia.org/wiki/Bulimia_nervosa* (scroll down under social)].

In a world lacking in love, and in a quest to be recognized, acknowledged, to fit in, and to belong, a desire to conform to a model celebrity image means that young people are losing themselves in the process. As adults we are no less involved, each image we see in a magazine, on television or on an advertising hoarding projects a certain ideal image that the desperate woman is trying to match.

The beauty trade is a multi-billion dollar industry: cosmetics, fashion, plastic surgery, gyms and spas, nail bars, fashion publications, modelling, beauty pageants and more if you take into account 'repair' clinics which have to deal with the aftermath of people resorting to drugs or other extreme means in an effort to deal with their intense disappointment in themselves and in a less-than-ideal world.

Weight management is important for good health but there is a world of difference between sensibly exercising self-control and being a compulsive obsessive. If you find yourself thinking too much about your weight, constantly looking in the mirror and feeling disgusted, or weighing yourself after every meal, then you have some inner work to do. If you can't accept yourself, then why should others? It's a dynamic which gives birth to a vicious circle.

Self worth comes from spending time with the self – do you care enough to sit and get to know your real inner self, or are you too busy looking in the mirror, and running away from who you think you might really be? Once we get in touch with our inner beauty through meditation, then we are less obsessed with the outer shell. In fact, as I begin to love and nurture my inner self then I am able to accept my physical self easily, even with its imperfections. I have understood what matters most.

Of course, the same underlying reasons of a lack of self-understanding and lack of self-love are also responsible for another scourge of society that is particularly evident in the western world, that is, the rapidly escalating incidents of obesity. It is the other side of a very uneven coin.

Emotional eating is the tendency to eat in response to negative emotions. Studies have shown that overweight individuals are more emotionally reactive, experience negative emotions and likely to overeat when distressed than people of normal weight.

The hunger that the overweight person is trying to fill is an absence of self love, self acceptance and self worth. It is an inner hunger that will never be satiated, and the person will always feel empty, no matter what. The need for comfort and the urge to self sabotage overpower the need for self control and discipline. If we look for these things outside of ourselves, then we will always be a slave to society's or to other people's opinions, and we can never feel fully happy with ourselves.

Thoughts are the seed of everything. If I am telling myself the story I am big, fat and ugly, then my life experiences will reinforce those beliefs. If I can revise my storyline to read I am special, I am beautiful, I am deserving, I am important and valuable, then life will confirm that back to me.

Of course these deep-seated beliefs will take more than a few affirmations to shift – and that is where meditation comes in. The first lesson in Raja Yoga Meditation teaches us that we are already beautiful and complete – we just need to connect with that inner beauty. As souls, we have all of the resources that we need within ourselves already, and the realization of this through deep understanding and experience is the secret to real self-esteem, self-worth and self-respect.

IT'S TIME… to finally understand that the body is simply our costume and an outer reflection of the inner being, and that beauty comes from within. When we rid our self of the negative baggage, we become truly light and 'weight-less'!

When we nourish those inner qualities the resulting sparkle of happiness, peace and contentment appear in a person's face, demeanour and attitude. This is authentic beauty!

Spiritual Bypass

The term 'spiritual bypass' refers to the avoidance or 'bypass' of healing and dealing with deep-seated soul issues under the guise of spirituality. One can wear the label of spirituality, walk the peaceful walk, talk the soothing talk, wear the right attire, shape the hair (or no hair), and yet continue to sweep the painful and unresolved wounds under the yoga mat. Spirituality can, if not understood properly, become a method of escapism.

Parents having problems dealing with their teenage children may spend more hours in voluntary community service than dealing with the concerns of their loved ones. For, to give advice to other parents is easier than to deal with the problems on your own doorstep.

Many paths advocate a degree of detachment in order to attain a certain level of spiritual enlightenment. This can become a convenient excuse for some to relinquish all personal responsibility towards those around them. For example, if it is my duty to provide financial and emotional support towards my family, and yet I am not there for them when they need me then that becomes detrimental to my spiritual progress and can become a hindrance in my prayer or meditation rather than an aid.

Some people mistake laziness for simplicity. Something they should be paying attention to, such as dressing up for the occasion or looking after their personal belongings becomes a chore and effort. These souls don't fully appreciate the beauty and royalty of spiritual simplicity and unnecessarily complicate their lives even more.

People may choose to stay celibate because they have problems dealing with intimacy and sexuality. They prefer to bury the subject rather than working through it.

Spirituality is meant to be a path of enlightenment and one which gives happiness. Don't confuse pseudo-spirituality with a genuine spiritual practice that involves real deep inner transformation. When spiritual principles are not applied properly, we are not tasting the happiness on the level it is promised. We are simply taking satisfaction from the aroma of the cuisine rather than eating and digesting it – where the nourishment lies.

Spiritual principles need to be digested properly, with understanding, in balance, in the right way. There is a fine but very important line between detachment and spiritual detachment, between laziness and simplicity, between charity at home and out in the world, between celibacy and pure love.

The path of spirituality is a path in which one finds one's own identity, which implies that we are all individuals and cannot be cloned. We cannot therefore copy others or their tracks and must be the pioneers for our own passage. If we are wearing other people's shoes then they may be too big or too small which will make us uncomfortable, and maybe even make us stop walking the journey altogether.

When one starts out on a spiritual journey, one is very often feeling powerful and happy because of the immediate rewards of the spiritual way of being, but like in any marriage the real work begins straight after the honeymoon is over. So too, after the initial highs and thrills of embarking on a new spiritual path, comes the realization that one must continue to invest time, energy and attention to keep achieving the same level, or an even higher level, of the spiritual returns.

We have the choice to bypass issues that may feel uncomfortable, but know that what you resist will persist and will need to be addressed at some later date.

It's Time... to Change

The avoidance and denial of deep issues creates the illusion of happiness and freedom and does not allow us to experience the ultimate soul freedom and happiness that is possible when we practice spirituality in the right way. Use spiritual knowledge to work through your issues and not as an excuse to bypass them.

IT'S TIME... to be honest with yourself, with no false pretenses, in which case you are only fooling yourself and no one else. Have the courage and determination to look under your yoga mat which includes your pain, guilt, regrets etc, because once they are removed the soul will feel so much lighter and happier for it. You will experience your real inner power and freedom, one that no one can take away from you. Then you can peacefully lie flat on your yoga mat – bump free!

Take Off Your Shoes

The removal of shoes before entering homes and holy places is common for many living in warmer climates. But is it just for hygiene reasons? What does this really symbolize? And why has this tradition been handed down from generation to generation?

Shoes, most often made of leather, are a metaphor for the physical aspect of the human being... the leather of 'body consciousness' so to speak. As I enter a mosque, a church, a synagogue or a temple, no matter how rich or poor, I cannot carry my ego or arrogance with me, even concealed in the cloak of my noble character... I have to leave all that at the door.

Body consciousness can come in many forms, for example being over concerned about the way I look (no wonder the beauty industry is a multi-billion dollar business) or needing to acquire (and show off) wealth and assets to 'keep up with the Joneses', i.e. to inflate my position in the eyes of others. In simple language, body consciousness reveals itself to us in some of the following ways: complaining, criticising, commenting, cursing, condemning, carping etc. Judgement, jealousy and a discontentment are very often the root of body consciousness.

The antithesis of this body conscious attitude would be 'soul consciousness'. Or, the antidote to this self-destructive behaviour would be the state of soul consciousness where I, the real self, am completely calm, cool, content and comfortable inside. A feeling of satisfaction and security comes when I understand that all of my authentic, invisible assets are within me; for it is from this place that my qualities of peace, love, joy, power, truth, creativity and compassion emerge.

In the eyes of God we are all equal and transparent; there is only a disparity in rank when we look at the body. All religions suggest that the body is merely a veil of mud or dust covering the soul, spirit, ruh, atma. Interestingly, the name atma, or atom comes from the Greek *atomos*, which means indivisible – something that cannot be divided any further. Thus, when we are stripped to our essence, we are free of any fancy labels, brandings or hallmarks of our heritage or education.

Similarly, as we arrive home, the act of taking off our shoes represents an un-layering – the transition of roles – from the variety of characters we play in our work place to 'becoming ourselves' once again.

Ironically, as we cast off the layers of ego that we have been comfortably hiding behind for so long, we become whole again. We are grounded, becoming one with our universal family. We accept ourselves, and can accept others for who they are. We can begin to appreciate their real qualities as we begin to see the light of the soul of each and every one behind their physical costume.

Light cannot be weighed against gold or diamonds, it is measured in attributes. It is the virtues (or lack of) in the soul that makes the soul shine (or dull). With every layer of body consciousness that we uncover, we reveal another tier of virtue in the soul.

IT'S TIME... to take off your 'shoes'. Get real. Be honest. Feel the ground upon which you stand. No need for masks or masquerades. In meditation, practice being conscious of the light of the soul and you will automatically discard the mantle of body consciousness. Similar to walking into a room; you do not attempt to chase away the darkness – you simply switch on the light!

The 'W' Perspective

The letter 'W' viewed from four different sides could give four very different meanings. Seen from different angles it can either be read as the number 3, an E, M or W. This just proves the point that four people sitting around a table will have at least four different opinions about the same situation. And the scary thing is... they are all right!

The perspective we 'choose' to take on any situation very much depends on our past experiences, our beliefs, our conditioning, our present mood and/or a multitude of other variables. The point is that, without stopping to consider another person's perspective, we so often think that we are 'right', and the other party is therefore invariably wrong.

We see this scenario played out everywhere, from school playgrounds to the world stage, often with disastrous consequences.

Our ego blinds us to the viewpoints of others. Our personal opinions become 'The Truth'. We insist on not removing the blinkers that keep us narrow minded and judgmental, and yet how often have we been made a fool when we find out that others can also be right?

It takes a great deal of humility and patience to view things from another person's perspective. How true is the saying, 'Don't comment on a person's life, unless you have walked a mile in their shoes'?

Learning to hold back, listen, consider, and respond thoughtfully are all important skills in maintaining relationships. What is more – as we hear it 'from the horse's

It's Time... to Change

mouth', we may even learn something new, find another way of doing things, expand our horizons, and at the very least begin to understand that everyone has something to offer and that rarely are things either black or white and there may be merit in a variety of options. Real listening is the basis of good communication, and ultimately good relationships.

To insist on talking when we should be listening, is not communication, it is dictatorship.

The fact that we have nearly 7 billion people in the world would imply that we have a minimum of that many opinions. Each human is a world unto themselves and has a right to their own opinion, perspective and belief. One might wonder then how it could be possible to create harmony in any relationship, or in the world.

An orchestra is an excellent example of harmony at its best. Each instrument is so unique and yet the sound that emerges from the collective is absolutely splendid. And furthermore, the more instruments the 'merrier' the music!

If we always engage in one-sided communications, then there will always be winners and losers. However, win/win outcomes are totally possible when we stay open and curious instead of closed and critical, and when we respect each other as a human being and an individual with individual ideas and points of view.

It is always possible to acknowledge and accept someone else's opinion without agreeing with it. This is the basis of conflict resolution – 'to agree to disagree'. Then the doors to real communication can open.

IT'S TIME... to stay open and to recognise that every situation has at least four differing perspectives and that I am only seeing one angle from where I am 'sitting'. Kill the ego and develop the humility to listen to another person's opinion without wanting to be 'right'. It might just well teach me something I needed to learn and give me a more clear picture of 'The Truth'!

Travelling Light

How many of us have longed for a journey away from our present reality, yet couldn't find the courage and determination needed to take that first step!

The first step is about challenging the known, and stepping into the unknown where there are risks to take and choices to make. Only then can we open ourselves up to adventures and pastures new. There is a famous Chinese proverb, 'A journey of a thousand miles begins with the first step.' Sometimes the first step is the hardest, but it's definitely the most important.

A spiritual journey follows a parallel road. It takes bravery and commitment, but it is the most rewarding journey of all.

In reality, when we travel by air, there is a weight restriction that forces us to define what we need. Anything over the prescribed amount is 'excess' weight, and for that we will be penalized.

On our spiritual journey we can easily be weighed down by too much 'luggage'. As we move along we continuously sift through the multitude of experiences, storing and building on what enriches our soul, but at the same time we may also be filling our soul suitcase with what is not so useful for our journey. It's always good to travel light!

If we are to 'stay light' or even 'fly' on our inner journey, it's important to be able to discriminate between what is necessary, and what will just hamper my progress. Learning to let go of what is not needed and keeping only what is important, takes wisdom and courage. As such, what we choose to take along and 'carry' inevitably defines who we are.

One of the joys of travelling is the sense of freedom that comes with it. As a traveller we let go of the burden of responsibility and instead become a visitor, a guest. As a guest we enjoy and take pleasure from the scenes in front of us, without getting caught up in the nitty-gritty details, knowing that each stop is temporary and that sooner or later we will indeed move on. We appreciate the moment without feeling we need to own it, and when it's time to leave, do so with sweet memories rather than the feeling that we need to hold on to anything. As we embark on our next step we reassess our direction, re-confirm our destination, and travel onwards, enriched by all that was learned at this stop.

On any journey we need to know our destination, and also how to get there. There is a saying: If you don't know where you are headed, you won't know when you have arrived! Thus, where exactly are we headed? What is our purpose, our aim and objective in life? Have we decided the route plan? Because if the destination is clear then our values are the compass that will keep us on track. For example honesty, self-respect, integrity and determination will carry us a long way. Happiness, satisfaction and contentment are the signposts that tell us that we are on the right road, and that the destination is not too far away. If the destination is not clear, the soul is lost and there is confusion; precious time is wasted.

With our spiritual journey, each realization brought into action is a step closer to our wholeness. Just as everything we observe and experience in different countries, cultures and climates adds to our knowledge and broadens our horizons, in the same way, every metaphysical experience we live through, whether 'good' or 'bad' is added to the photo album that becomes our character. Just as we select the best pictures for the album, are we also careful in choosing and displaying our best qualities and moods?

No matter how many miles you travel across the globe and how many oceans you cross, the ultimate journey is the internal one – the journey to inner space, and inner peace.

Check what is in the suitcase of your soul. Is it heavy with grudges, resentments, worries, doubts and negative and destructive thoughts? If that's the 'case' then you will definitely be stopped at customs! And so, if there is a barrier, burden or blockages that is stopping you from moving onto your next adventure declare it i.e. 'clear' it with honesty and cleanliness.

IT'S TIME... as you travel to the inner recesses of your being, discern those thoughts that allow you to travel lightly, and discard those that weigh you down. Take time to reflect on how these affect you, how they shape you and how they impact on your relationships. Decide on your destination. And then pack your bags well, for you don't want to arrive and find you have forgotten your most valuable piece/peace!

Understanding Death

The question of what happens next when we let go of this 'mortal coil' is a topic for much theory and speculation, but little hard fact, for obvious reasons!

For some it can be a cause of great fear and anxiety. For others in certain circumstances it may represent a welcome release, for yet others there may be the realisation that there is actually little to be afraid of and more to look forward to!

Our condolences go to Steve Jobs family. He was a genius, a visionary, and a tech-guru, who changed the lives of many millions. Tempted by that juicy apple so long ago, the life of Adam and Eve and of mankind changed forever. In a more benign but equally alluring way... the Apple of Steve Jobs' creation has transformed the way the world functions today.

For someone who passed away a billionaire, the first lesson he teaches us is that no one carries away even a penny into their next destination. The physical wealth we earn and accumulate is just for this lifetime. Wealth is only meaningful if you use it wisely and enjoy it while you are still alive and kicking.

It is the fragrance of good times and the fruit of the good actions you have created in this lifetime that will be carried away in the suitcase of your soul; it is the blessings you have earned from others and the Divine that will travel with you; and it is the seeds of good karma (deeds) sown that will continue to serve you in the future.

Over 2000 years before Jobs, Alexander the Great also taught us a similar lesson. On his deathbed he made three requests. Firstly he said, 'Let my hands hang out of the coffin so all can see that I am taking nothing with me. Despite all the lands I have conquered … I came empty handed and I am leaving empty handed'. Secondly, an instruction to 'Have all my wealth – gold and silver – strewn after my coffin so people know it is a waste to chase after it'. And thirdly, 'Have the physicians carry me – to prove that even they cannot save this body from the clutches of death!'

Raja Yoga meditation teaches us that death is not an end to our existence. In the sheer experience of 'soul consciousness' – the awareness of the true self – we realize there is no death, only life, for the soul is eternal. No fire can burn the soul, no water can drown the soul, and no knife can cut the soul. I, the soul, or spirit, am eternal and imperishable. I never die. As I deepen my experience of my true essence, (as opposed to the false sense of self – a body conscious attitude) then fear dissolves and I become more able to live life to the full, enjoy the present moment, and experience a deep sense of peace and security. I know beyond doubt that I am eternally loved and protected.

Each time I tune into myself as a soul and detach from my physical surroundings, including mentally detaching from my own body, I have an experience of what it means to disengage from the material world. The more I am versed in this feeling, the less fear there will be of dis-connecting when the time comes to part and 'disentangle' from this body.

There are thousands of reports by people who claim to have had a 'near death' experience. Their testimonies are surprisingly consistent. The vast majority felt a great peace without any fear, and a deep sense of one-ness with all Creation. Their most powerful experience was a sense of being loved so fully and unconditionally, like nothing they had experienced before in 'life'. So beautiful were these experiences that many did not want to return to this world. When they did, their lives were often transformed, and all fear had dissolved.

For some who have time to prepare for death due to a long-term illness, it can be a time to forgive and forget, to make amends, and to prepare for the inevitable. It can be a time of realisation, reconciliation and peace. Yet others can spend their 'last days' full of regret and remorse, crying over a life unlived. How a person perceives the final chapters of their life to be in this case depends upon the mindset of the individual, and what one chooses to do with that precious time.

If one has traveled through the journey of life with honesty and integrity, there is no need to worry about the next stop. There is fear when there is unfinished business – with moral debts owing and accounts with others 'in the red'.

Yes, one day we will leave behind our loved ones, of that there is no doubt. Therefore, let me do the work now to transform my attachments into real love, to live a life of giving rather than taking, and to leave behind a legacy of a life spent joyfully, purposefully and lovefully.

IT'S TIME... to embrace death as the next step in the journey of life, to understand it as a beginning rather than an end. Close all debts with love and forgiveness. Don't spend time chasing after things that cannot be carried away in the suitcase of your soul. Pack only sweet memories and you will travel 'light'!

Lifting the Veil of Illusion

Illusions are a false or misleading impression of reality. They are experiences that are created by our own mind that confuse our senses. We are led by our own mind to believe one thing and in actuality it shows up as something else. How do we recognize and escape the emotional illusions, to see the reality behind them before we are tricked or misled, and how do we free ourselves from the pain of being fooled or cheated?

Illusion is sometimes described as Maya. In Hinduism Maya is the principal deity who manifests, perpetuates and governs deception. She is depicted as a female, a temptress, luring and enticing the individual away from truth (note: both male and female can be lured, not just the male!). And once the individual is entrapped, Maya reveals her true evil form. The word Maya comes from a Sanskrit root *ma* ('not') and *ya*, ('that'). So Maya is literally that which is not!

Illusions are often referred to as a veil as they distort or blur our vision – we can't see the thing for what it really represents. Even if we can see the form, we can't see the true colours. We only see the illusion, through the veil, and what it wants to show us and not otherwise. It takes a great deal of courage to remove the veil to see what is really behind it. One may prefer to stay in the comfort zone of remaining blind to the truth, and that is one's choice.

By choosing to remove the veil, we are choosing to wake up. Otherwise the illusion lulls us into a deep perpetual sleep. It feels pleasant and comfortable. We may not realise that it is Maya's job to numb the senses, to prevent us from seeing and feeling something deeper, more rich, colourful, powerful or perhaps painful.

It is better to wake up gently and willingly than with a jolt! Sometimes life experiences can shake us so hard, it is only then we see the truth, the truth we have been avoiding looking at for so long. Surely it is better to explore, investigate, research the outcome of our thoughts before acting upon them. Waking up can be precipitated by the comments of others because they can often see beyond our blind spots more clearly than us – if only we can have the presence of mind to accept what they say. However, they can only shatter the illusion if we have the humility to listen, saving us from the pain and distress that Maya, the illusion, may bring.

Only knowledge and understanding can dispel Maya. Knowledge is light and Maya is the darkness. Darkness is simply the absence of light. Illusion is the rope that we mistake for a snake in the darkness. The illusion is crushed once the rope is revealed. In the same manner, once we have an insight into a certain feeling or emotion, we realise it was not real, just a projection.

These days there are 3D, 4D and even 6D movies that use different sensory perceptions to imitate reality. 'Real life' is no different – where our emotions overtake our sensibility. We think we are happy until something comes along and takes that happiness away, which is when we realise it was not real happiness but based on something temporary and illusory. However, the truth is the soul is happy – always. And not only *after* I receive the bunch of flowers!

We live off many illusions that feed the self-image in the wrong way! We mistake wealth for happiness, anger for control, ego for confidence, lust or attachment for love and so on. And we don't even realize that Maya the illusion makes us into our own worst enemy by shielding us from the truth and as a result creating more sorrow. We are innately powerful, abundant and complete with all beauty, yet Maya plays hard to hide this truth from us.

It takes a refined intellect to discriminate truth from falsehood. Nowadays everything false looks so real – fruits, jewellery, even wax idols in Madame Tussauds – that it's hard to know which is the real thing. Likewise, people also play with our feelings – advertisers try to prove how good their product is and how we won't be complete without it, health firms try to promote their products as a cure-all, restaurants try to entice us with 'the best meal in town', and lovers promise to give us everything!

Maya the chameleon knocks on our door in various forms. We are led astray like the innocent Red Riding Hood, only to realise later how far we have come from 'home'. We then need a compass to get back. It is the compass of Truth that we need to find.

Truth is constant – it never changes. Truth enlightens. Truth brings joy not sorrow. Truth guides the soul. Truth is value and principal based. Truth is our original pure self, and once we act from these inherent qualities we can never be deceived.

IT'S TIME... to remember that all that glitters is not gold! To learn to recognise the illusion before the pain kicks in. Ask questions to seek the truth behind the matter – the insight and wisdom of the answers should eventually make us peaceful, removing all restlessness. When we realise deeply how powerful and abundant we are within our own right, we will never open the door to Maya again!

The Birth of Desire

Many great thinkers, including Socrates, have argued that individual desires must be postponed in the name of a higher ideal. Is this so and what is it about the object of desire that is so luring and tempting?

Marketing and advertising companies have researched this subject thoroughly – some present us images of desirable figures and personalities, while others leave us feeling we are lacking in something. And we are gullible as there is not the power to stand alone and be different and unique!

If unbridled desire were such a good thing, then why do we use expressions such as, 'This (desire) is driving me crazy', or 'I'm going mad' or 'I'm losing control'. Desire itself or the pursuit of it is not always looked upon as a prudent and sensible goal. Rather, it is mostly perceived as a weakness. Perhaps it's due to religions scaring us with the deadly sins but then again perhaps not!

Maybe it is truly our own inner aversion toward our own lacking, emptiness, thirst and craving that induces the soul to act out of (spiritual) line. Desire makes us a slave, a peasant, a beggar and we dislike this in ourselves; very akin to a king who has forfeited his kingdom and now finds himself having to beg, knowing deep inside that this is not his original nature.

In fact, it would be fine if desire arrived alone, but no! It comes with a coach-full of other uninvited guests – jealousy and possessiveness are the 'parents' to first descend onto the pavement (of our lives)! Scientists are still unsure how to define jealousy in its entirety. They do know that it is 'a protective reaction to a perceived threat to a valued relationship'. This perceived threat could be with any of your following Ps: people, power, prestige, pennies, pay, position or possessions.

Thus jealousy is a secondary emotion; a reaction to something happening underground such as competition and comparison; the negative thoughts and feelings of fear and insecurity are mostly the culprits. That is why we engage in the pursuit of the object of our desire. Because the desire is not satiated until the soul 'owns' and has full control over the object (one of the Ps!). This introduces possessiveness and ownership.

We have met the parents of desire – how about its progeny? Anger, greed, attachment, ego and lust are the offspring of desire.

In order to protect that possession we hold onto it tightly – this is called *attachment*. Then we feel perhaps more of 'it' will make us feel better and *greed* is born. When greed is not enough (because it is never enough… is it!?), then we get *angry*. And in order to protect our honour in the face of society, I develop an *ego*, trying to be something or someone I have not quite been able to achieve practically. Finally even that is not soul fulfilling and I lust after my desire. These five negative traits, like our five fingers, have the ability to grip the soul.

The point at which this becomes pain, is when after having pursued these desires, we have completely lost sense of feelings. This is quite a paradox, since the initial idea, urge or wish etc. originated from wanting an optimum experience from the root of the desire. Yet by the end of its cycle our senses have become numbed. And like a drug, we need more and more each time to fulfil that appetite. In relationships in particular, when desire has overtaken the soul, it undermines genuine love and respect. In the name of love we manipulate, and in the name of respect we control. We are no longer sensitive to people's needs, just caught up in sheer selfishness.

Excessive desire has often been described as sin. Sin simply means to 'miss the mark'! Thus when any virtue has gone wrong, it has missed its mark – its original purpose and intent. I miss the mark when I use anger to control rather than being at peace with the situation. I miss the mark when I get attached and want to hold on, rather than love and let go. I miss the mark when greed grips me in the illusion that I will be happier when I have more. I miss the mark when ego tries to convince me that that is the real/true me! I miss the mark when I lust after things and not my pure essence.

Everything about desire is associated with the fostering of 'I' and 'mine'. It all begins with a single thought related to 'I', the identity, or 'mine', the extension of 'I' in terms of people and possessions. In fact we only desire in a state of emptiness. In a state of fullness there is no more space needing to be filled.

You may ask where ambition fits into this equation. Are we to give up all drive and passion and become 'aimless wanderers'? Ambitions should motivate and energise us. A desire almost always harasses, distresses and exhausts us. There is a place for ambition in our lives, so long as it respects our true essence and others. The gage would be, if my success is achieved at the expense of others that cannot be ambition that is desire. Not to say all ambitions are pure, as some may not be detrimental, but definitely have selfish motives (which would then fall into the category of not respecting others)!

If there is such a thing as positive desires, then it has to be of the highest order; one that brings me closer to my perfection and not takes away from it. If there is a desire pulling me down, there is a greater one compelling me towards my inner excellence – let us stop to listen to that inner voice.

But whether it's desire or ambition, either way we need to learn to let go of expectations. We should put in the effort but thereafter need to accept the outcome. That's when we can truly say we have transcended desire i.e. gone beyond personal preference such as like or dislike. Very often when we let go of wanting something badly, that's when the universe very often delivers it to us; almost as if it was waiting for us to learn the lesson of letting go and accepting the flow.

IT'S TIME... to aspire to our highest goal of perfection, one that is free from desire. Let go and embrace the flow. Check that the soul is operating out of virtue and not weakness. Now that the king has regained his memory, it's time to reclaim all rights and not beg. And then I can send that whole coach-full back into oblivion!

Honesty is the Best Policy

If a picture paints a thousand words then the camera paints volumes! With the increased use of mobile phone cameras people everywhere are maximizing their liberties and taking footage of the latest alarming war crimes, or documenting teacher-student conflicts in schools, or recording unsanitary mobile food vendors and their concealed, repulsive habits. With evidence in hand, everyone from government officials to street hawkers are being asked to be more responsible and accountable.

Some people wonder if values matter anymore since certain individuals seem to be ascending the rungs of fame and swiftly crossing wealth brackets despite their lack of morals and ethics. But generally it is only a question of time 'before one gets caught in the act'; if not by the judicial system or the media, then surely by the moral expectations of fellow citizens. Losing the trust, approval and esteem of fellow friends and customers, has to be the harshest sentence one can experience.

The Stephen Covey Foundation surveyed 54,000 people and asked them to identify the essential quality of a leader; integrity was by far the number one response! Since humans have the ability to choose, they have a greater responsibility toward the world.

All systems – family, economic, political, social — fall apart because of a lack of honesty and integrity! How do you feel when you find out your partner is being unfaithful or your children have been lying to you about their whereabouts? What is your initial reaction when you find out your staff have been embezzling or siphoning off company money? How do you feel when the politician you voted in turns out to be a crook? How do you react when you know your doctor is suggesting further treatment just to make some extra money!

Trust is broken and moreover we feel deceived, betrayed, cheated and angry. We are angry more so with ourselves than others – for trusting, for caring, for believing, for being naïve and gullible! Along with that our ego is also dented because we have to admit to ourselves that you we were incorrect in our judgment and for investing trust and confidence in those figures. In fact our arrogance and pride do not allow us to be honest, only our humility does.

Honesty is priceless; it is a noble quality and a form of self dignity. It overrides all other weaknesses. You may even decide to pay more for an honest housemaid, cashier or employee even if their other credentials do not fit the job description! And when they return to you the extra change they got or are not tempted by your material 'stuff' your respect for them shoots up even more.

Honesty is indeed the best policy. To tell one lie means to have to tell another hundred to cover it up! And so in this you are allowed to be too lazy to lie – because keeping up with the lies takes extra effort and attention, which is best left to other greater pursuits. In court the judge and jury always take into account the honest confessions of lawbreakers and the sentence is lightened. In life too, if we are honest, we will most likely be forgiven.

Yet, what stops us from speaking the truth? Is it fear: of being let down, or what others may think of me, or of hurting others? Of course, as adults we go to great lengths to protect our image and our egos, and of course there are ways of being honest that do not wound others. But these are skills we must learn in order to respond to life's many challenges and maintain a certain level of personal honour and dignity.

In reality more damage is done when we are NOT honest. In the guise of being polite and pleasant we withhold truth purposefully or simply by remaining silent. Silence does not mean consensus. This kind of silence only misleads others and ultimately hurts their feelings! Don't we appreciate people when they give it to us straight? For example, 'I won't be coming to the dinner evening.' Or the boss to the employee: 'You're a fantastic employee, but I am going to have to let you go, as I can't afford to keep you.' When we are honest with people, they trust us! They admire us and better appreciate us; in return we are able to get more of what we want.

However, spiritual honesty advocates that we be honest with ourselves first, rather than making life convenient for ourselves and expecting others to change, let me go inside and check where it is that I need to change. And even God is pleased with someone who is honest and pure at heart.

We forget that when we pick up one end of the stick, we pick up the other also. So, as we are allowed to be honest, so are others! I need the capacity and courage to hear their truth.

Children get what they want because they ask for it! This is one of their most attractive qualities. There are no hidden agendas; simply a pure heart, an innocence of spirit… and surprisingly we find this charming.

IT'S TIME... to take responsibility for your life and actions and become more accountable. You will win love and respect and be showered with blessings if you stay humble and use honesty as your policy. Honesty is a noble quality and adds value to our soul. When you act with this courage, then all eyes and cameras can be on you and there is absolutely no need to fear!

In God's Heart

One of the few places we go to find rest and comfort when we are troubled and distraught is into God's heart. His heart is warm and welcoming, cozy and comfortable and safe and secure. All faiths remind us to remember Him, not because He *needs* us to! But so that as we re-member, and re-connect with His divine and mighty qualities we begin to vibrate in His same frequency of love and light.

God is the one Being that everyone remembers at a time of need – why is that so? Perhaps because, buried in the inner recesses of our soul, there is a memory that 'Once upon a time…' God liberated us from all our pain and sorrow; showed us a 'way out' of our troubles? Even an atheist will remember God at some point; perhaps at death, or even if it is to prove the non-existence of God! Whom do we remember when we are down and out? Those who have given us a helping hand, showed some sympathy and walked that extra mile for us – we never forget them.

We also remember God because He has performed magic and miracles in our life in a way that no human being can. God has His unique ways of shielding us from further harm, guiding us at the right time, empowering us to face any eventuality, and creating opportunities in disguise. He is the One soul who is always looking out for us and will never let us down.

In human relationships one of the major mistakes we make is of handing over our heart to loved ones and expecting them to take over God's job of being a miracle worker! We trust fully, giving them access to our whole heart. In desperation we continue in the relationship believing that one day, that chosen one will heal all old wounds and remove past hurts. But when, for whatever reasons, our needs and wants do not get met, or that trust gets betrayed, we get upset and blame that one for not being a 'professional heart repairer'! And then fight the long battle to get our heart back. But surely this is a tall order to ask from someone who themselves are also most likely injured and in search of the same 'professional'! Simply put, give others your love, not your heart.

With so many broken hearts being nursed today, it is only God, the Supreme Surgeon who has the patience and tolerance to sew together the broken pieces of our heart. Only God's love is the soothing balm that pacifies the soul; His light, a fine laser healing our wounds. And for any healing to take place effectively, the patient needs silence and solitude. Too much sound and action will only aggravate the wound and perhaps even delay or halt the healing process. Time is also the greatest healer – no healing can or should be rushed.

The intimate connection we seek with human beings is in actual fact the souls yearning for the ultimate experience of this Divine connection. In that meeting between God and I, nothing matters, time and space fade away and it is as though I have arrived 'home'… this moment is eternally cherished in the immortal soul.

After tasting this divine, pure, altruistic and unconditional love of the Supreme once again, we realize how foolish we were to run after human love. God is the Ocean of Love and His love never depletes. And in case anyone thinks that it's God's role to punish us for our sins then they have misunderstood Him. Yes, if He punishes, He 'punishes' us with His love – 'kills' us with His love so to speak! He showers such immense love on us that we totally melt in that fire of love, all the alloy of ego and impurity melt away and we are returned to our original blueprint – our true essence. That is how God transforms, with love and not pain.

After discovering this 'Lovemine' of God's pure love it is important to return frequently to fill up the tank of the soul. In a state of fullness and abundance it is easy to be generous, but when we have a limited stock, it makes us misers.

IT'S TIME... to sit in God's cozy Heart and to allow Him to be your Healer! Take back custody of your own heart. Soak up the beauty and magic of God's love. Give God a chance, by understanding His delightful and intriguing ways and means. Know and trust that He is always there guiding and protecting you. And when your heart is fully mended and you are the sole owner of it, even God will invite Himself in.

About the author

Aruna is fortunate to have the blend of both cultures – the East and West! She was born in Nakuru (Kenya), educated in London (England), worked in Vancouver (Canada), and has lived in various other parts of the world and travels regularly to India.

Aruna was exposed to spiritual truths from an early age; in fact she had her first meditation experience at the tender age of 8. By the age of 14, she had found her calling and decided to focus on what mattered most in life– the development of her soul journey. For the past 36 years, Aruna has been studying the gentle art of Raja Yoga Meditation taught by Brahma Kumaris World Spiritual University (www.brahmakumaris.org). She is currently one of their experienced teachers, travelling regularly to promote the work of the university, running retreats, managing projects, teaching and facilitating in the areas of human development and writing weekly articles.

She has also helped establish meditation centres in Canada, Turkey, Bahrain and Kuwait. Aruna is a Certified Negotiator in Conflict Resolution and together with her education in natural health continues to promote a peaceful, natural and vegetarian lifestyle.

To learn more about It's Time Blog go to:
www.arunaladva.org
or email: info@arunaladva.org.

About the Brahma Kumaris

The Brahma Kumaris is a network of organisations in over 100 countries, with its spiritual headquarters in Mt Abu, India. The University works at all levels of society for positive change.

Acknowledging the intrinsic worth and goodness of the inner self, the University teaches a practical method of meditation that helps people to cultivate their inner strengths and values.

The University also offers courses and seminars in such topics as positive thinking, overcoming anger, stress relief and self-esteem, encouraging spirituality in daily life. This spiritual approach is also brought into healthcare, social work, education, prisons and other community settings.

The University's Academy in Mount Abu, Rajasthan, India, offers individuals from all backgrounds a variety of life-long learning opportunities to help them recognise their inherent qualities and abilities in order to make the most of their lives.

All courses and activities are offered free of charge.

Visit www.brahmakumaris.org for more information.

How and where to find out more

SPIRITUAL HEADQUARTERS
PO Box No 2, Mount Abu 307501, Rajasthan, India
Tel: (+91) 2974-238261 to 68
Fax: (+91) 2974-238883
E-mail: *abu@bkivv.org*

INTERNATIONAL CO-ORDINATING OFFICE & REGIONAL OFFICE FOR EUROPE AND THE MIDDLE EAST
Global Co-operation House, 65-69 Pound Lane,
London, NW10 2HH, UK
Tel: (+44) 208-727-3350
Fax: (+44) 208-727-3351
E-mail: *london@brahmakumaris.org*

REGIONAL OFFICES

AFRICA
Global Museum for a Better World, Maua Close,
off Parklands Road, Westlands
PO Box 123, Sarit Centre, Nairobi, Kenya
Tel: (+254) 20-374-3572
Fax: (+254) 20-374-3885
E-mail: *nairobi@brahmakumaris.org*

AUSTRALIA AND SOUTH EAST ASIA
78 Alt Street, Ashfield, Sydney, NSW 2131, Australia
Tel: (+61) 2-9716-7066
Fax: (+61) 2-9716-7795
E-mail: *ashfield@au.brahmakumaris.org*

It's Time... to Change

THE AMERICAS AND THE CARIBBEAN
Global Harmony House, 46 S. Middle Neck Road,
Great Neck, NY 11021, USA
Tel: (+1) 516-773-0971
Fax: (+1) 516-773-0976
E-mail: *newyork@brahmakumaris.org*

RUSSIA, CIS AND THE BALTIC COUNTRIES
2 Lobachika, Bldg. No. 2, Moscow 107140, Russia
Tel: (+7) 499-264-6276
Fax: (+7) 495-261-3224
E www: brahmakumarisru.com
www: spiritual-development.ru
E-mail: *moscow@brahmakumaris.org*

www.bkpublications.com
E-mail: *enquiries@bkpublications.com*